Descriptosaurus Personal Writing

T0300042

Descriptosaurus Personal Writing provides young writers with an opportunity to link their personal lives and school experiences, and gives writing a meaningful and personal context. It is a resource that will guide and scaffold students to produce vivid, powerful, descriptive and meaningful personal texts, and, acting as a springboard for other genres, will dramatically improve the quality of their writing in all areas.

It provides a detailed step-by-step guide through the writing process by using personal narratives to develop the skills, knowledge and understanding of writing a text. It demonstrates different techniques, and provides useful tips and suggestions on how to revise a text and transform it into a powerful, descriptive personal narrative. With prompts, plans, methods and models for poetry and prose, this book helps tackle each stage of the writing process from planning and writing a first draft to revising and editing.

Descriptosaurus Personal Writing is an ideal vehicle for welcoming and celebrating different cultures, experiences and stories into the writing curriculum: an invaluable resource to dramatically improve children's writing for all KS2 primary and KS3 secondary English teachers, literacy coordinators and parents.

Alison Wilcox developed *Descriptosaurus* as a resource for her own teaching to scaffold and develop children's creative writing, with dramatic results. The first *Descriptosaurus* book was published in 2009, and following its success, Alison gave up full-time teaching to research and write. Alison is now involved in several research projects, including working with the United Kingdom Literacy Association (UKLA) and the World Education Summit; working with schools to develop new resources; and conducting workshops for organisations, teaching alliances and schools.

"Are you looking for ways to support personal writing? This accessible book is packed with ideas to help young writers use their memories, feelings and experiences and lean on their lives. This will help to support their development as writers and build a writing community in your classroom. A community of diverse and engaged writers."

Teresa Cremin, Professor of Education,
The Open University, UK

"Supporting young children to write their own personal story can be one of the most enjoyable acts in all of teaching. And yet, young children require ample support to find their voice and to craft a compelling narrative. Alison Wilcox, in her book, *Descriptosaurus Personal Writing*, offers teachers a brilliantly accessible resource to help with that challenge of supporting young writers. By offering purposeful prompts, exciting exemplification, along with accessible guidance, Wilcox provides teachers with a timely tool to help grow great young writers."

Alex Quigley, author of *Closing the Reading Gap* and *Closing the Vocabulary Gap*

Descriptosaurus Personal Writing

The Writing Process in Action

Alison Wilcox

Routledge
Taylor & Francis Group

LONDON AND NEW YORK

Cover illustrations: Dani Pasteau

First published 2022
by Routledge
2 Park Square, Milton Park, Abingdon, Oxon OX14 4RN

and by Routledge
605 Third Avenue, New York, NY 10158

Routledge is an imprint of the Taylor & Francis Group, an informa business

British Library Cataloguing-in-Publication Data
A catalogue record for this book is available from the British Library

Library of Congress Cataloging-in-Publication Data
Names: Wilcox, Alison, author.
Title: Descriptosaurus personal writing: the writing process in action/
Alison Wilcox.
Description: Abingdon, Oxon; New York, NY: Routledge, 2022. |
Includes bibliographical references. | Identifiers: LCCN 2021034717 |
ISBN 9781032105079 (hardback) | ISBN 9781032105116 (paperback) |
ISBN 9781003215653 (ebook)
Subjects: LCSH: Creative writing (Elementary education) |
Literary form–Study and teaching (Elementary) | Narration (Rhetoric)–Study and teaching (Elementary)
Classification: LCC LB1576 .W487594 | DDC 372.62/3044–dc23
LC record available at https://lccn.loc.gov/2021034717

ISBN: 978-1-032-10507-9 (hbk)
ISBN: 978-1-032-10511-6 (pbk)
ISBN: 978-1-003-21565-3 (ebk)

DOI: 10.4324/9781003215653

Typeset in Myriad Pro
by Deanta Global Publishing Services, Chennai, India

Contents

Acknowledgements and dedication   viii

Introduction   **1**
The aim of the book   4

1 The writing process   **7**

2 Making learning in the writing process visible   **12**
Teachers as coaches in the 'writing community'   13

**3 Personal narrative writing: a springboard for other forms
     of writing**   **17**
Personal narrative: a springboard for other genres   18
The power of poetry: a stimulus for other writing, a vehicle for
       expression and practising the writing craft   18
Re-purposing personal narrative writing   22
Persuasion   23
Other ideas   23
Final thoughts   24

4 What is personal narrative?   **26**
Elements of personal narrative writing   26

5 Getting started: a writing journal   **28**
First thoughts: who are you?   30

6 Prompts   **39**
Memory list prompts   40

7 External sources as writing prompts   **45**
In the news   45
1. Social media: friend or foe?   47
2. Racism in sport: show it the red card   50
3. Action for climate change   53

8	**Plot outlines**	**58**
	Simple six-question outline template	61
	Simple six-question outline model	62
9	**Writing a first draft**	**64**
	Rehearsing the story orally	64
	Writing the first draft	64
10	**The revision process**	**67**
	Caution	69
11	**Revising action scenes**	**70**
	Using slow-motion technique to build suspense	70
12	**Setting**	**76**
	Describing an object, scene, landscape	77
	I would really like to go back to …	82
	First Morning in Corfu	85
	Setting as part of a personal narrative	88
13	**Characters**	**92**
	People watching	92
	Character planning: *Rusty the Dog*	94
	Using a photo and dialogue: *Alfie Misses Out on a Piece of Bacon*	95
	Character investigations	96
	Developing the skill of 'show not tell': *Rusty the Dog*	97
	Innovating a character description	99
	Developing the skill of 'show not tell': *Mr Rogers*	101
	Mr Rogers (*Science: Tales of Torture*)	102
	Second draft: *Discovering a Writing Journal*	103
14	**Dialogue**	**106**
	Dialogue tags	106
	Action beats	108
	Revision	109
15	**Reflections**	**110**
	Reflection starter	110
16	**Editing**	**112**
	Tips	112
	Editing model	113
	Editing punctuation	114

Appendix   **117**

Writing survey template
Writing survey model
The writing process from published writers
Modelled sentences: detail, flow, impact (DFI)
Rusty the Dog: a memoir
The Terrier Times
Mr Rogers: Science: Tales of Torture
Science: Tales of Torture: Messages
First Morning in Corfu
Sunrise on Corfu
Rwy'n Gartref [I am home]: description
Stunning Staycation: The Gower Peninsula
I'll Call Mammy
Floodland: Found Poem by Alison Wilcox, drawing from the novel
     by Marcus Sedgwick
The Sock Thief: A Moment of Frustration
Negativity in the Media: An Angry Response
Spider's web planning template
Scene/image box plan template
Scene/image box plan model
Fiction planning template
Fiction planning model
Character prompt card
Alison's Book Club
Research, articles, books and websites

Acknowledgements and dedication

To my family for their patience and understanding when I disappear into "Narnia" and my world of fiction; and to my two dogs, Alfie and Monty, for listening so attentively when I try my poems out on them. To Claire Rigby for all your support and enthusiasm.

Thank you to Liz Brownlee, Sue Hardy-Dawson and Charles Finn for giving me permission to use their powerful, thought-provoking poems. To the National Literacy Trust, FE News and RSPH for allowing me to include extracts from their thought-provoking articles and research papers, and to Greater Manchester Police for providing me with the statement they issued on 31 January.

As always, thanks to Bruce Roberts and Molly Selby of Routledge for their continued support, guidance and wisdom, and to the UKLA for asking me to deliver a Personal Narrative workshop at their national conference, the response to which was the stimulus for the writing of this book.

For any apprentice writer to improve, the first step is honest reflection. Many thanks to Jenson for your honest and courageous reflection in the writing survey. Your determination to improve and your consequent progress has been a delight to see.

To Madeleine Lindley, thank you for letting me loose in your wonderful book centre and, as always, for your expertise and guidance in directing me to some fantastic texts.

Introduction

In the Annual Literacy Survey 2016 (NLT), Clark and Teravainen examined the impact of writing for enjoyment on attainment (Clark and Teravainen, 'Writing for Enjoyment and its Link to Wider Writing,' June 2017), and found that 'there is a clear relationship between writing enjoyment and writing attainment … nearly eight times as many children and young people who do not enjoy writing write below the expected level compared with those who enjoy writing.' The report concludes: 'Overall, the findings highlight the importance of writing enjoyment for children's outcomes and warrant a call for more attention on writing enjoyment in schools, research and policy.'

In addition, in the NLT survey in 2017, Clark and Teravainen investigated the link between reading and writing enjoyment and mental wellbeing. The report found that there was a link between positive attitudes to writing and mental wellbeing: 'children and young people who enjoy writing very much and who think positively about writing have, on average, higher mental wellbeing scores than their peers who don't enjoy writing at all and who hold negative attitudes towards writing' (Clark and Teravainen-Goff, 'Mental wellbeing, reading and writing,' September 2018). Commenting on this new research, Jonathan Douglas, director of NLT, added,

> We now know that reading and writing for enjoyment can also play a vital role in helping children lead happy and healthy lives. Our latest National Literacy Trust report, *Mental wellbeing, reading and writing*, found that children who enjoy reading and writing in their free time have significantly

DOI: 10.4324/9781003215653-1

better mental wellbeing than their peers who don't … an enjoyment of reading and writing can help children develop literacy skills they need to take control of challenging situations, which is particularly important when children are feeling vulnerable. It can enable children to make sense of how they're feeling, express their thoughts and emotions and seek support when they need it.

Research by the Department for Education (DFE-RR238) demonstrated that the teaching of writing is effective when pupils are taught about the writing process. In its new framework, the Office for Standards in Education (Ofsted) confirmed the need to give pupils ownership of their writing, including choice of what to write, with a focus on incorporating pupils' own lives into the writing curriculum. In addition, there is an expectation that pupils demonstrate their ability to revise and edit their own work.

The aforementioned research supports the need for a resource that not only demonstrates the writing process but does so in the context of personal writing projects, which is the aim of this book.

A way to engage pupils in developing and enjoying their writing is to give them ownership of that writing: to give them a choice of what to write; how to tackle the writing process; to explore and experiment, and eventually, discover their writing voice and style; and be able to adapt what and how they write to suit a variety of purposes and audiences.

It is widely accepted that giving pupils the opportunity to write about what interests them, their own lives, and what is important to them gives pupils a meaningful context in which to write, and results in improved engagement, enjoyment and the quality of the writing, as the pupils have a vested interest in the task rather than one merely set by a teacher or adult.

Personal writing provides pupils with an opportunity to link their personal lives and school experiences, and to use writing to connect these two areas of their lives. It gives writing a meaningful and personal context.

The increase in enthusiasm for writing in some schools when they were closed due to the Covid pandemic has been insightful. From initial impressions, it would appear some pupils found that they had more time to spend on a piece of writing, more choice about what to write, and a more obvious link between writing and their homelife. Hopefully, all schools will be able to take advantage of this increased enthusiasm and maintain that link between school and home writing.

The increasing use of class blogs is an exciting development that widens the audience for the pupils' work from a geographical perspective and enables them to access a variety of readers of different ages, backgrounds and cultures. It gives the writing real authenticity and purpose and has had a positive effective on pupils' attitudes to writing. Some of the platforms facilitate 'personal journal spaces' for the pupils to develop their ideas and thoughts privately and to 'work on the craft of being a writer'; others enable pupils to engage with their learning community and share and discuss the writing they are working on at home (quadblogging.net). Some schools have even reached out, via their blogs, to professional writers, who have enthusiastically shared their practice and processes, and opened the pupils' eyes to the process of writing by giving them an authentic and exciting 'real world' perspective. (Some quotes by professional authors about their writing process and links to interviews are included in the Appendix.)

Blogging, however, is an area where there are still some issues that need to be 'ironed out.' For example, apart from the obvious need to educate pupils about online safety, the availability of computers in the classroom, rather than the disruptive and time-consuming practice of having to decamp to an information and communications technology (ICT) suite (access to which is limited), is a problem in many schools. In addition, adherence to all the stages of the writing process is not being consistently applied, so some content is posted without an editorial element.

Blogging is a popular and successful way of promoting writing in the United States, Australia and Canada, and hopefully with additional funding will become a way of engaging young writers in the UK (Myra Barrs and Sarah Horrocks, 'Educational Blogs and Their Effects on Pupils' Writing,' 2014).

A writing survey template is included in the Appendix. This is a good way to initiate discussion with a new group (or individuals) about their attitude to writing, their perceived strengths and weakness, the way they currently tackle the writing process and the strategies they use. A survey completed by a young teenager I have been working with is also included in the Appendix, which is enlightening and demonstrates the value of these discussions with pupils: to use their interests and passions as a starting point and as valuable feedback about what areas require additional support.

THE AIM OF THE BOOK

The aim of this book is to provide a resource for pupils, teachers and parents that guides them step-by-step through the writing process: how to tackle each stage (brainstorming, planning, writing the first draft, revising and editing) with prompts, plans, methods and tips, and models for personal narrative, poetry, persuasive texts and newspaper articles.

Narrative texts are generally the most popular choice for reading at home, by both parents and pupils. As it is the form of writing that pupils know most about, and are most comfortable and confident with, the book uses personal narratives as the vehicle to illustrate the writing process. It is the easiest form for pupils to 'mine for ideas' and develop writing content, as the people, places and experiences are already familiar to them. This familiarity and confidence with the content and form of personal narrative writing makes it an incredibly lucrative and effective first step to guide pupils through the various stages of the writing process. It allows the focus to be firmly on acquiring, practising and applying the essential skills and knowledge to understand what constitutes a powerful and effective piece of writing, and what steps or strategies individual pupils need to adopt at each stage of the process to develop and improve their own writing.

Whilst the book focuses primarily on the writing process in the context of personal narratives, it also demonstrates how the content, skills and knowledge can be 'repurposed' to develop an understanding and application in different forms of writing, for example, persuasive, informative, reflective and descriptive. In addition, the book demonstrates the power of poetry to express and craft new ideas and content, and how it is a powerful stimulus for other writing.

The book is also designed to support and guide teachers to write alongside their pupils. The benefits of teachers writing with pupils to provide a platform for discussing the writing process are well documented. This modelling enables the teacher to demonstrate their thought processes and the strategies they use as they put their ideas down onto paper, then revise and edit them, and is invaluable to deepen pupils' understanding. Struggle and challenge are a vital part of the learning process, and it is, therefore, important that young writers witness first-hand an adult writer experiencing the same or other challenges, obstacles and hurdles, and then observe how the adult writer tackles and overcomes these challenges and what sort of strategies they adopt. It helps young writers gain an understanding of the writing process and, through modelling, discussion and exploration, to find the method that best suits them.

Adults writing alongside young writers helps them to understand that most experienced writers work from a rough first draft, and then rearrange the structure of the content, develop the description and detail, and craft powerful, interesting and vivid sentences during the revision process. Well-structured, developed, descriptive writing and original sentences rarely emerge from a pen or a keyboard without hard work and a willingness to experiment, add, delete or substitute in the revision and editing stages of the writing process.

Families talking about writing by discussing shared memories, experiences etc. is also incredibly beneficial, and this book is accessible for families to use to work on a home writing project, such as a family memory book.

In recent times, many families have struggled with the demands of home-schooling, and some have found it difficult to support their child's literacy at home. Even with little previous experience, knowledge or perhaps confidence, parents, carers and extended family members have a vital role to play to develop their child's writing. Taking time to share memories – retelling stories of past holidays, journeys, events, celebrations, traditions, rituals, people and places – is an important first step and can be an extremely positive and bonding experience. This discussion enables young writers to collect ideas and build a 'bank of writing content.' Using oral storytelling is an excellent way to engage the whole family, make them feel part of a writing project and write about their culture, background and experiences. It is an opportunity for young people to learn about their roots as part of their journey to becoming a writer. **Talk** is the first and a vital step in the writing process.

Working together to write these stories as a family memory book or even an annotated family photo album is a fun and engaging shared experience. It is also a way of making writing meaningful. Apart from a more positive engagement with the writing task, there will also be a demonstrable improvement in the quality of the writing.

In the rest of the book, pupils are referred to as 'apprentice writers' because it is important that they view themselves as writers developing their 'writing craft,' as part of a 'writing community' where there are experienced writers available to guide and coach them through the process.

1

The writing process

Composing texts involves a sequenced, step-by-step process, from generating ideas to publishing a finished piece of writing. Understanding the stages in the writing process gives apprentice writers a clear mental map of the steps they need to take to produce a piece of writing which fits its purpose and engages the reader. It develops their skills in both their authorial (the drafting and revision) and secretarial (editing) stages. It makes **visible** each step in the process of crafting a text, the strategies that can be adopted at each stage, and, with effective feedback given at each step, it scaffolds the writing task. It helps to develop an apprentice writer's self-efficacy – the confidence to tackle a piece of writing by believing in their ability, and that, through their own efforts and the strategies they adopt, they can improve their writing.

The writing process involves the following stages:

1. AUDIENCE AND PURPOSE

* Why am I writing this?
* What am I writing?
* Who am I writing it for?

DOI: 10.4324/9781003215653-2

2. BRAINSTORMING IDEAS

- ★ Events
- ★ Places
- ★ Characters
- ★ Key moments
- ★ Key ideas
- ★ Information about a topic

3. PLANNING AND REHEARSING

- ★ Sorting ideas
- ★ Developing ideas, plots, descriptions
- ★ Organising ideas, information, themes
- ★ Rehearsing the writing: retelling the story aloud to an audience, who ask questions about any information, events etc. that are unclear

Each writer has a preferred method of planning. Some like a boxed plan, others story webs or illustrated storyboards. Some like to just get their ideas down on paper without much planning; others prefer to plan in a methodical, detailed way using an outline for each element of the story (setting, character, plot, problem and resolution) or topic. It is important to explore each method to find which one suits each individual writer.

4. DRAFTING

- ★ Recording ideas in a first draft

Very few professional writers get the draft 'right' the first time, and many rewrite their text dozens of times. They see the draft as a time of discovery: a small step in the writing process. It is a testing ground to explore ideas and decide:

1. What you want to write
2. How you want to write it

The blank page is the first major obstacle any writer needs to overcome. *There is nothing but white space staring back at you.* The best way to overcome this is to ignore it and just start writing words: even one word on the page means it is no longer blank. Freewriting is a useful strategy to 'open the mind' and helps overcome the 'blank page syndrome.' A freewriting exercise is included in Chapter 3.

5. REVISING

Improving the effectiveness of the writing:

★ Whole text
★ Sentences
★ Word choice

Professional writers do not regard first drafts as failures or a sign that they cannot write. In fact, they don't expect them to be particularly good, but instead see them as a step along the writing journey: a stage that leads the writer closer to their final destination – publication!

> **Step 1:** Does the organisation of the text convey its meaning and aid understanding?

Re-seeing the text as a whole – its organisation, structure and development of detail – helps us to assess whether its message, idea or theme is fully developed, clear and complete so that it assists in understanding its purpose, and its content and construction engage the reader.

> **Step 2:** What does each sentence or phrase add to the overall effectiveness of the text?

A. SENTENCE LEVEL

★ Does the sentence make sense?
★ Does it aid the flow of the writing, or is there a lack of variety in how the sentences are started, or the type and length of the sentences?

For example:

★ Does each sentence start the same way?
★ Are they all simple sentences?
★ Are some of the sentences too long and, therefore, confusing?
★ Is the length varied to build highs and lows and vary the pace of the writing?

Zoom in to examine each line to assess what it adds (or detracts) to the effectiveness of the text.

B. WORD CHOICE

★ Are the verbs powerful and varied?
★ Is good use made of specific nouns, adjectives, expanded noun phrases and figurative language?

A good place to start is to identify words that are repeated often throughout the text and develop a bank of appropriate synonyms. Modelled sentences demonstrating key strands in the writing curriculum are included in the Appendix.

The final stage adds the final touches and 'polishes' the text ready for publication.

6. EDITING (PROOFREADING)

Check:

★ Spelling
★ Grammar
★ Punctuation

7. PUBLICATION

Assessing the effectiveness of:

★ Presentation and layout

Making sure:
★ Handwriting is legible

At this stage, the text is being prepared for sharing with an audience.

2

Making learning in the writing process visible

The key to learning is making progression visible.

> ★ Where am I now? How does my work compare to what I am trying to learn?
> ★ Where to next? How do I close the gap between where I am and where I need to be?
> ★ Where am I going? What am I trying to learn?
>
> John Hattie

Progress can be demonstrated by recording the history of a piece(s) of writing in a folder where the improvement in the text through the entire writing process can clearly be seen, as can the strategies used. At the end of the year, apprentice writers can assess their progress by selecting a text written in the first term of the same academic year, and using the skills, techniques and strategies learned throughout the year to rework it into a more effective piece of writing.

Apprentice writers also need models to be able to visualise where they are and where they need to go. Keeping writing from previous years (with the names blanked out) is an ideal way of providing a variety of models for them to use. They are also useful for modelling the revision and editing process.

DOI: 10.4324/9781003215653-3

TEACHERS AS COACHES IN THE 'WRITING COMMUNITY'

Whether it be sport or writing, a coach will initially demonstrate (model) the skill and technique to be mastered; design and model the activity or routine to practise that skill; identify the ultimate performance goal and describe and discuss the 'game plan' (process) to achieve the desired outcome.

At times, when things are not going as well as planned, it is necessary for the athlete to return to the coach for further feedback and different strategies or adjustments to their technique to continue their improvement. But, think about examples of the most successful sportsmen and women, and how they have achieved their goals. Whilst it is vital that the coach scaffolds the athlete's progression and it is essential that the athlete understands the steps they need to take, it is then the response of the athlete and the effort they are prepared to commit that will ultimately guarantee their success. Michael Jordan (one of the most famous and successful basketball players of all time) attributed his success to his belief that:

> If you put in the work, the results will come … Never say never because limits, like fears, are often just an illusion.
>
> Michael Jordan

It is, therefore, essential that apprentice writers enjoy writing, actively participate in the learning process, and are fully engaged and committed to making progress.

Writing 'coaches' model the skills and techniques required at each stage of the writing process, and then scaffold the 'practise' of that skill or technique by inviting the apprentice writers to interact on a shared writing task. This can be done by asking them to assist in the decision-making process, for example, by asking some of the questions in the following list.

EXAMPLES OF QUESTIONS FOR GUIDED WRITING

★ Which idea do you think comes next?

★ How do you think we should say that?

★ Do you think we should start a new paragraph for this? Do any of our other ideas go with this one?

★ Do you think the reader will understand what we meant here? Does it make sense? If not, how should we amend it?

★ Have we checked that we have said everything?

★ Have we repeated anything?

★ I'm not sure that word is spelt right. How should it be spelt? How can we work it out?

★ Can you think of a better verb?

★ Should I join these two sentences?

★ How do you think I can add that extra detail? Should I use brackets?

The apprentice writer, like the aspiring athlete, then practises the skills and techniques, focusing on those areas that need improvement and using the routines and strategies modelled. When necessary, they seek feedback on how to improve a skill or to apply a different strategy that will assist them in their progress towards their initial performance outcome and, eventually, to becoming an 'expert writer.'

Like the aspiring athlete, it is of the utmost importance that apprentice writers develop a 'growth mindset' (Carl Dweck) and are helped to understand that their progress in writing (and all areas of life) depends on their understanding that '**mistakes, struggle and challenge are essential elements in the learning process.**' Instead of thinking, '**I'm bad at writing,**' coach them to change their mindset to one where they reflect on:

1. What went wrong?
2. What do I need to improve?

3. Who can I ask for help and feedback?
4. What strategies can I use to help me?

Instead of thinking, 'There's no point. Why bother?' coach them to change their mindset to one where they embrace the challenge, accept that there will be obstacles to be overcome, and take a reflective approach by asking what they and others can do to help them make progress:

1. Any mistakes I make are a first attempt at learning.
2. I need to ask for help when I need it.
3. I need to slow down.
4. I need to put in more effort.
5. I need to practise harder and work on those areas I need to improve.
6. I will learn to do this.
7. I can improve.
8. I will improve.

Progress can and will be made, the current abilities and talent of apprentice writers can and will change over time if they embrace this approach of identifying the areas that need improving (with the assistance of an experienced writer), accepting that success and failure are part of the learning process and have a determination to work on those areas. How many times have you seen repeated comments on an apprentice writer's texts advising them to check their full stops and commas? Taking an approach outlined earlier and developing strategies with the teacher during the editing stage of the writing process, apprentice writers seek feedback to correct any misunderstanding of sentence construction, rather than persisting with the same misconceptions year after year.

In his inspirational book *The Learning Rainforest,* Tom Sherrington describes the trouble he had with creative writing:

> The feedback was always so unhelpful. 'B minus. The ending is rather corny.' More like a stinging review than constructive guidance for improvement.

What was I meant to have done differently? There was no chance to improve it and we'd move on. Retrospective feedback was the default. I don't think I ever got an A. For me, there was too much 'hit and hope' in English literature and creative writing. You never knew exactly what to do. In fact, my whole experience of learning poetry was of feeling that everyone else was in on a secret that I was too stupid to understand.

Having read Tom's inspirational book, and greatly admired his writing style, I can only say, 'What a shame! The world lost out on a future writer of exceptional science fiction (a genre he enthusiastically engaged with as a young student).' It's never too late, Tom.

3

Personal narrative writing

A springboard for other forms of writing

Apart from providing a **record of events** and experiences in young people's lives, personal writing is a means to **reflect on** and **clarify** those important moments and experiences. They are a vehicle to help them **understand** and **respond to** the things that have happened to them or are going on around them, both for a 'public' or 'private' audience. It is an opportunity to 'download' thoughts and feelings.

They are also an ideal vehicle for welcoming and celebrating different cultures, experiences and stories into the writing curriculum. Sharing these diverse narratives demonstrates that every individual's experiences and cultures are valued, and promotes understanding, acceptance and appreciation by their peers.

Through an area which motivates apprentice writers to enthusiastically put pen to paper (fingers to the keyboard) because it is relevant to their lives outside school and therefore makes them more invested in the quality and improvement of their writing, four major skills are learned and developed which will aid their ability to write in a range of forms and for a variety of purposes and audiences: planning and organization, mechanics (sentence structure, grammar and punctuation), and development of vocabulary.

DOI: 10.4324/9781003215653-4

PERSONAL NARRATIVE: A SPRINGBOARD FOR OTHER GENRES

Many apprentice writers tend to approach a personal narrative by simply listing a series of events, with little description of places or people, personal thoughts and feelings, and no reflection on how the event impacted on their lives: what they learned, gained, understood or how it changed them in some way. This book is a resource that will guide and scaffold apprentice writers (young and old) to produce a vivid, powerful, descriptive and meaningful personal narrative, and will dramatically improve the quality of their personal writing as well as have significant benefits for other aspects of their writing.

In personal narrative, the apprentice writers are focusing on the writing craft, as they do not have to create new events, characters or settings, but merely develop their observations and descriptions. They have first-hand experience of how they felt and what they thought and did, so it is also an ideal vehicle for exploring the technique of 'show not tell,' and reflecting on the experience. They can explore the pacing and flow of their narrative through experimentation with different sentence structures, openings and lengths. At various stages in the writing process, they can self-assess or use a peer or adult writer to discuss the effectiveness of their writing craft to communicate their story, and then make any identified adjustments and improvements during the next stage of the process.

The skills, knowledge and understanding of the writing process and the 'writing craft' developed through personal narrative act as a springboard for other forms of writing where these skills can be transferred and developed in a different context. For example, the development of close observation skills and the ability to include detailed description is an important, transferable skill acquired during personal narrative writing instruction, which is equally important in other curriculum areas, such as history, science, art and geography.

THE POWER OF POETRY: A STIMULUS FOR OTHER WRITING, A VEHICLE FOR EXPRESSION AND PRACTISING THE WRITING CRAFT

Poems are included throughout the book to stimulate discussion and writing. In addition, a list of poetry books is included in the Appendix.

Introducing apprentice writers to a wide range of poems will demonstrate their value as a vivid, powerful and effective form of expression, and a fabulous source of descriptive treasures. Poetry is also an incredibly effective form to practise the 'writing craft' (as well as improving vocabulary), as in a **poem every word counts**. As poems do not involve large amounts of texts, they also encourage experimentation and risk-taking.

> Poetry matters because it is a central example of the use human beings make of words to explore and understand. Like other forms of writing we value, it lends shape and meaning to our experiences and helps us to move confidently in the world we know and then to step beyond it.
>
> *Teaching Poetry in the Secondary School: An HMI View*, HMI (1987)

In every young life, every young writer, there is a defining moment: an experience, a thought, an emotion; a line from a poem, song, rap or book; a text or comment on social media. It is important that apprentice writers are taught how to capture that moment, and poetry is a perfect vehicle to enable them to find their voice to do so and to express their feelings about themselves and their world.

Research has shown that developing the ability to recognise, understand, manage and share a wide range of emotions, challenges and anxieties helps children and young people on a journey of self-discovery that builds resilience and provides strategies to manage their mental health, which has never been more important than in the current climate following the Covid pandemic and the concerns about managing the mental wellbeing of young people as a result of their experiences in such challenging and uncertain times.

Allocating time to discussing issues of emotional wellbeing in schools has been proven to be a reliable indicator of academic achievement, improves behaviour in the classroom, reduces incidences of bullying and results in significant improvements in mental health.

Jonathan Douglas, director of the National Literacy Trust, commented:

> Children and young people today face a multitude of pressures at school, at home and in their social lives. It is imperative that we do everything we can

to enable our children to develop the resilience they need to cope with life's challenges – and our latest research shows that the joys of reading and writing can be highly beneficial.

Not only does a love of reading and writing enable children to flourish at school, but we now also know it can play a vital role in supporting children to lead happy and healthy lives.

Poetry is an ideal medium due to its short, concise format, which makes it more accessible to readers, especially reluctant or struggling readers, or those for whom English is a second language, and thus enhances confidence and motivation in reading and writing. It helps young people make a personal connection to literature and its rich, imaginative language.

The concentrated focus of poetry on a theme or emotion can be the key to opening a conversation, to promote discussion and establish a pathway to honest reflection in a safe, trusted and stimulating environment. For example, the following poem *You're Not on Your Own* can be used to introduce discussions about people or organisations to turn to in a time of need, and as a stimulus for writing an innovated or invented poem about who the apprentice writer could and would look to for support. (An innovated model, *I'll Call Mammy*, is included in the Appendix.)

When young people discover that the poems can speak to them, their lives, their emotions and their experiences, these poems will encourage them to identify more enthusiastically with poetry and the emotions and events described in them. Poetry provides an opportunity and stimulus for apprentice writers to share and write about themselves, their feelings and important events in a supportive, collaborative community of writers where taking risks is not only acceptable but welcomed.

The synthesis of imaginative and personal writing provided by poetry means that it is an effective platform for developing emotional literacy as well as improving motivation, engagement, enjoyment and success in writing and life in general.

YOU'RE NOT ON YOUR OWN

My voice is drowned out,
by the noise in the room.

I may be quiet; appear strong.
But I have feelings; I have worries.
I care; I cry.

Don't be fooled by the mask.
Don't be taken in by the silence.

If you cut me, I will bleed.
I get wounded by your words.
I get bruised by your actions.

I replay those words.
I relive those actions.

When I am on my own –
When I am in bed
When others share **their** thoughts.

But who should I turn to?
Who can I turn to?
Who will listen to me?

It's okay to be vulnerable.
It's okay to make mistakes.
It's good to share your worries.

There is always someone there for **you**.
There's always someone who will listen.

Tell me where you're hurt.
Tell me about your wounds.
Tell me where you're bruised.

I care.
I'll listen.
I can help; I will help.

Take the first step.
Talk to me.

You're not on your own.
By Alison Wilcox (2019)

RE-PURPOSING PERSONAL NARRATIVE WRITING

Writing is a complex process of interrelated skills that need to be understood and practised until they become automatic and can be applied fluently to a piece of writing. For example, an apprentice writer who struggles with spelling will exhaust much of their limited working memory on figuring out that particular element of writing, and often then lose their flow of ideas, as will those who lack a fluency in their handwriting. Apprentice writers who cannot compose, punctuate or manipulate a simple sentence with ease will struggle when adding more complex elements and details. Writing about familiar content allows the focus to be directed to new skills and knowledge that need to be learned, to practise essential transcription skills, and to develop an understanding of the various stages of the writing process.

Developing an understanding of each stage of the writing process and the various knowledge and skills required through an initial focus on personal narrative can then be transferred to a form or content that is less familiar. It is important to provide opportunities for apprentice writers to experience a range of forms of writing, for example, description, persuasion, expression; or instructive, informative and explanative (poems, recounts, letters, leaflets, brochures, guides, posters, slogans, instructions, reports).

When apprentice writers 'fall short of the mark' on a particular piece of writing, the problem can sometimes be attributed to a difficulty in expressing and structuring the unfamiliar content of their text. Re-purposing a narrative or a poem, where the content is already familiar and developed, leaves the apprentice writer to focus on the form of the new piece of writing: the structure, style and language features appropriate to this new form.

For example, the Appendix includes a model of a newspaper article where the story *Rusty the Dog* has been repurposed; informal messages by witnesses to the *Swivelling Tap Incident*; two poems crafted from the original description in *First Morning in Corfu*; and a persuasive piece highlighting the delights of the Gower Peninsula to persuade the reader to visit the area on a staycation, adapted from the poem *Rwy'n Gartref*, which has already been repurposed for a descriptive, reflective text.

PERSUASION

Persuasive writing is an important and very engaging form, which most apprentice writers tackle with great enthusiasm. It incorporates vital features, structures and language that are extremely useful for all aspects of written communication.

Apprentice writers have usually mastered the verbal art of persuasion, so are already aware of many of its features, for example, emotive language, repetition and rhetorical questions. There are many aspects, issues and conflicts arising in the home and school that lend themselves to an authentic purpose and real audience for personal persuasive writing. For instance, negotiated screen time, household chores, pocket money, curfews, homework assignments, assessments, to name but a few. These issues can be treasure trove for writing activities in school and at home.

OTHER IDEAS

1. The social media reflection in Chapter 4 can be developed into a persuasive piece, with parents as the audience, and the purpose to persuade parents to lift a fictitious or 'real' ban on using social media following a widespread campaign warning of the dangers to young people's mental health of social media; or a discursive text examining the advantages and disadvantages of having a social media profile, with evidence and examples.
2. Use the *Rwy'n Gartref* model and write a poem for your local area. Repurpose it into a description and then an information leaflet describing the area and places of interest, landmarks, festivals, celebrations etc.
3. Repurpose the poem in this chapter, *You're Not on Your Own*, for a personal poem about someone who is always there to listen, help and offer support. (A model is included in the Appendix, *I'll Call Mammy*.)
4. Use the poems in Chapter 4 to write a poem about racism or climate change. Use a text, for example, *Floodland* by Marcus Sedgwick, to write a 'Found Poem.' An example is included in the Appendix.

a. Repurpose the poem on racism to write a letter or blog supporting the **Show Racism the Red Card** campaign (https://www.theredcard. org/education-pack).

b. Repurpose the poem on climate change to write a leaflet to inform parents or the local community about the threat of global warming and the need to take urgent action.

c. Repurpose a description, for example, *First Morning in Corfu*, and craft a poem that 'lifts out' elements of the description. (An example of a haiku and a cinquain are included in the Appendix section titled "Sunrise on Corfu.")

d. Repurpose a personal narrative to produce a script or comic strip.

FINAL THOUGHTS

If we want young people to be engaged and enjoy writing, it is essential that we give them the opportunity to use their own life – their experiences, reactions and feelings. *Air* was written in the hope that all apprentice writers will one day have the space and time to give *their words air* and discover their pens moving faster and faster across the page in their enthusiasm to write about something that truly matters to them.

(The majority of the texts included in this book are my models, which has made it easier to break down and illuminate the writing process. There are, of course, an abundance of fabulous examples that can be used as writing models, and a number are included in "Alison's Book Club" in the Appendix.)

AIR

Deep inside me,
thoughts and words
remain unspoken,
remain unwritten:
gasping for air,
aching for light,
waiting for me
to find my voice.

Given space and time,
my pen roams,
meanders, then gallops,
faster and faster
across the page.

By Alison Wilcox (2019)

4

What is personal narrative?

* The purpose of personal narrative writing is to capture a moment, an event, a reflection, a reaction, a thought or feeling.
* Personal narrative writing provides pupils with the opportunity to **relive and reflect on an event or experience from their own life** or from events in the world around them.
* A **memoir** is a specific type of personal narrative writing that examines the **meaning of a writer's life during a specific moment in time**.
* Apart from providing a **record of events** and experiences in apprentice writers' lives, personal narrative writing is a means to **reflect** on and **clarify** those important moments and experiences. They are a vehicle to help writers **understand** the things that have happened to them.

ELEMENTS OF PERSONAL NARRATIVE WRITING

* Introduces a **place**, **person**, and an **event or experience**.
* Includes information about **WHO**, **WHAT**, **WHERE**, **WHY** and **WHEN**.
  Note: Sometimes the memory is about:
  * **A place** (**WHO** may not be relevant)
  * **A person** (**WHERE** may not be necessary)
* Key events are written in **chronological order**.
* Includes **thoughts** and **feelings** of the **writer** during the event.
* Develops **details** of the event with **description** and **action**.
* Develops **characters** with **physical description** and **dialogue**.

DOI: 10.4324/9781003215653-5

★ Uses **vivid verbs**, **sensory details** and **figurative language** to create a **mood** and **tone**.

★ If personal writing is a ***memoir***, it **closes with a reflection**.
What was the value of the experience? What was:

  ☆ Learned

  ☆ Gained

  ☆ Understood

  ☆ Changed

5

Getting started

A writing journal

> Writing is an extreme privilege but it's also a gift. It's a gift to yourself and it's a gift of giving a story to someone.
>
> Amy Tan

All young people should be introduced to the benefits of writing and provided with a writing journal. They should be given the time and space to write, to reflect on events, to recapture important moments, people and places. A writing journal can be a place to reflect on their learning journey, and the content, processes, struggles and challenges they meet and how they have overcome them.

Many young people will discover aspects of themselves in this powerful and thought-provoking poem, *Please Hear What I'm Not Saying*, by Charles Finn. A writing journal gives apprentice writers a place to take the first step, to 'remove the mask': a safe place to express their thoughts and feelings.

DOI: 10.4324/9781003215653-6

EXTRACTS FROM *PLEASE HEAR WHAT I'M NOT SAYING*

Don't be fooled by me.
Don't be fooled by the face I wear
for I wear a mask, a thousand masks,
masks that I'm afraid to take off,
and none of them is me.

***

Pretending is an art that's second nature with me,
but don't be fooled,
for God's sake don't be fooled.
I give you the impression that I'm secure,
that all is sunny and unruffled with me,
within as well as without,
that confidence is my name and cool-ness my game,
that the water's calm and I'm in command
and that I need no one,
but don't believe me.

My surface may be smooth but my sur-face is my mask,
ever-varying and ever-concealing.
Beneath lies no complacence.
Beneath lies confusion, and fear, and aloneness.

But I hide this. I don't want anybody to know it.
I panic at the thought of my weakness exposed.
That's why I frantically create a mask to hide behind,

So I play my game, my desperate pre-tending game,
with a façade of assurance without
and a trembling child within.
So begins the glittering but empty parade of masks,
and my life becomes a front.
I tell you everything that's really nothing,
and nothing of what's everything,
of what's crying within me.

So when I'm going through my routine
do not be fooled by what I'm saying.
Please listen carefully and try to hear
What I'm not saying.
What I'd like to be able to say,
what for survival I need to say,
but what I can't say.

By Charles Finn (1966)

'It is only the back of an old exercise book from the last school year, but it's somewhere I can write, I can think, I can remember; somewhere I can remove the mask, somewhere I can be me.'

Alison Wilcox, *Discovering a Writing Journal*

Keep a notebook. Travel with it, eat with it, sleep with it. Slap into it every stray thought that flutters up in your brain. Cheap paper is less perishable than grey matter, and lead pencil markings endure longer than memory.

Jack London

FIRST THOUGHTS: WHO ARE YOU?

Reflecting on who you are; what matters to you; fears, loves, hobbies etc is a good place to start a personal writing project. Following are four autobiographical poems which provide outlines and a creative outlet to consider *who you are*. The templates can also be used to develop a character outline of friends and family to build a complete picture of you as an individual and the important people around you. They can also act as 'memory triggers.'

Who is Alison Wilcox?
* Main character trait (giggler)
* What you love (dogs, sport)
* What you fear (rats, lightning)
* Places you would like to visit (Peru)
* Someone you would like to have met (Jane Austen)

My Colours

Use the colours of the rainbow to represent what is important to you.

I Am Grateful

Develop a list poem of things for which you are grateful:

* ★ Things you hear, see, smell, feel
* ★ Friends, teachers, family, home
* ★ Trips, places
* ★ Books, music, clothing, inventions

My Song

Explore how different moods can be reflected by the music you listen to and what images or memories they create. Using similes and a variety of senses (sight, touch, smell, sound) is an effective way of painting a vivid picture of how that music makes you feel; what it reminds you of.

WHO IS ALISON WILCOX?

A giggling scribbler, news-watcher, bookworm.
Mother of Robert and Kitty; wife of Andrew;
Lover of dogs, comedy and sport,
Who feels happy, excited, determined;
Who fears rats, lightning and blindness;
Who would have liked to have met Jane Austen;
Who would like to visit Peru;
Resident in the magnificent hills of North Yorkshire.

By Alison Wilcox (2019)

MY COLOURS

(based on a poem by Colin West)

These are
my colours –
one by one:

Red –
the dragon
the fiery emblem of my nation.

Yellow –
daffodils
worn proudly on my lapel on St
David's Day.

Green –
the hills and valleys
of my homeland.

Blue –
the sea
where I stand and dream.

Violet –
the wildflowers
blanketing my secret wood.

Pink –
my favourite
vivid, vivacious shoes.

White –
a blank page
full of possibilities.

My rainbow of colours –
together
they make
a rainbow of me!

By Alison Wilcox (2019)

I AM GRATEFUL

I am grateful for these three things I hear:
Birds chirping in my trees at first light.
Laughter in my kitchen.
The sound of waves crashing onto the shore.

I am grateful for these three things I see:
The strip of orange as the sun rises.
The daffodil buds breaking through to trumpet the coming of spring.
The crystal patterns frosting the leaves and grass.

I am grateful for these three things I smell:
Freshly brewed coffee first thing in the morning.
The smell of roasting chicken announcing the promise of a family dinner.
Scents of pine, cinnamon and nutmeg at Christmas.

I am grateful for these three things I touch and feel:
The silky soft feel of my dogs' fur.
The tickle of grass on my bare feet.
The warm glow of an act of kindness.

I am grateful for these three animals and birds:
My two loyal Labradors.
The pheasants that strut across my lawn.
The magnificent elephants I met in South Africa.

I am grateful for these three friends:
My husband who has been my soulmate for twenty-five years.
My college friends, Gail and Brenda, with whom I have shared a lifetime of memories.
My son and daughter who love me as I am.

I am grateful for these three teachers:
Mrs Taylor who challenged me, inspired me and championed me.
Mr Lewis who made me reflect on how to inspire a love of writing.
Miss Thomas who gave me a life-long love of sport.

I am grateful for these three family members:
My parents for whom there isn't a mountain they wouldn't climb to be there for me.
My husband whose belief in me is limitless.
My children, who I love as my offspring, and like and admire as wonderful young people.

I am grateful for these three things in my home:
My enormous bed on which I can star-fish at night.
My office, Narnia, a magical world through my wardrobe.
My kettle, which is always in use.

I am grateful for these three trips:
Camping trips with my family to discover a love of the outdoors.
The trips to La Cala – sun, relaxation and BOOKS.
The trip to South Africa to immerse myself in the beauty of the wild.

I am grateful for these three books:
Little Women, which inspired a desire to write.
Pollyanna, which taught me to remember to be grateful.
My Family and Other Animals, where I can immerse myself in the wonderful descriptions.

I am grateful for these three character traits:
Humour
Empathy
Determination

I am grateful for these three things I like to wear:
My worn-out walking boots for tramping up the hills.
My pink shoes that make me smile when I look down.
My bobble hat that keeps my ears warm on a rugby touchline.

I am grateful for these three inventions:
The internet, which gives instant access to information, entertainment and communication.
My automatic washing machine, as I remember my mum standing for hours over a twin tub.
My central heating, as I remember the icy breaths each morning when I emerged from the cocoon of my blankets.

Whenever I feel down and gloomy,
I write a list of three things,
For which **I Am Grateful.**

By Alison Wilcox (2020)

MY SONG

My song can be like the misty dawn of a brand-new day;
Or like a dazzling rainbow after a storm.

A shimmering haze of pastel colours;
Or an explosion of orange on the horizon.

My song can sound like an acoustic guitar strumming in the shadows;
Or like a brass band in the market square.

It can feel like a rain shower massaging a tired body;
Or like an electric pulse in my veins.

My song can move like a wave sliding onto the beach;
Or like a puppet jerking on a string.

My song smells like a roast chicken in the oven;
Or like an aromatic, spicy curry.

It can be a soothing symphony of solitude;
Or a firework of exploding joy.

My song,
depends on
how I feel.

By Alison Wilcox (2020)

Using poetry to explore enjoyment of a time of day/daily routine

* Pick a daily routine or your favourite time of day.
* Break it down into steps, actions – think of it in slow motion.
* Make a note of words, phrases of sights, smells, sounds, actions, feelings or thoughts.
* Develop your notes into a poem or a personal description.

COFFEETIME

Tap, tap, tap, tap beats the pen.
Kettle starts to sing.
Ginger biscuit hums along.
Chair starts to swing.

Lid's percussion joins the pen.
Shake, rattle and roll.
Aroma wafts around the room.
Perfume for my soul.

Chair reclines – savours the taste.
A sensory safari.
Lubricates a rusty mind,
To a turbocharged Ferrari.

By Alison Wilcox (2019)

Journals have many uses, including capturing a moment, an observation, or a scene by jotting down words and phrases which can be used later and developed into a piece of writing. An example of a few pages from a writing journal can be found in Chapter 8.

The following poem and quote illustrate why using a writing journal is a valuable tool to develop writing.

REMEMBER TODAY

WRITING JOURNAL

What did you see today?
What did you learn?
When you saw the rim of pale pink,
Peek through the clouds.
How did you capture the new dawn?
Will you remember it another day?

When you watched the sun
Slide away again below the hills,
And night spread across the sky
Will you remember what you saw today?
Will you recall what you learned today?

Stop a moment.
Look closely.
Take it all in.

Jot down what you see and hear.
Jot down what you learned.
Capture your thoughts.
Notes in a Journal.
To help you remember –
What you saw and learned today.

By Alison Wilcox (2019)

Preserve your memories, keep them well, what you forget you can never retell.

Louisa May Alcott

6

Prompts

Many young people assume that their lives are boring; they have nothing interesting to write about. The first step is to open their eyes to the wealth of material (the gems in their own lives) that can be used as a stimulus for writing.

Apprentice writers often find a blank page daunting. The prompts in this chapter are a useful source of inspiration from which they can draft a 'memory list.' This will provide ready-made ideas for current and future writing projects, and can be added to as more events and experiences are remembered.

Sometimes a memory comes to mind quickly, but when you start trying to develop it, it proves to be disappointing as there is not enough material to make it interesting. This often happens to apprentice writers, who come with an idea, start writing enthusiastically, only to discover that they quickly run out of ideas. Writing a list gives an excellent source of material, and should one memory or idea prove to be disappointing, there is a ready-made list of others to turn to.

Judith Kerr, the author of *When Hitler Stole Pink Rabbit,* an autobiographical account of her family's escape from Berlin and the Nazis, gave an insightful interview for the BBC Radio 4 Bookclub (www.bbc.co.uk/sounds/play/b050z2vc). She talks about what prompted her to write the book, her reservations about whether anyone would be interested in reading her story, and whilst she tried to write as truthful a record of the journey as possible, how she added details from her imagination to fill in the gaps in her memory or to make the story more dramatic. This interview would be encouraging and inspirational for any young writer.

DOI: 10.4324/9781003215653-7

MEMORY LIST PROMPTS

Think of an important event in your childhood when you:

A. **Learned a valuable lesson that changed you in some way**
B. **Felt one of the following emotions:**
    * Betrayed
    * Jealous
    * Angry
    * Sad
    * Happy
    * Excited
    * Anxious
    * Nervous
    * Appreciated
    * Grateful
    * Misunderstood
    * Embarrassed
C. **Something that has an important memory associated to it**
    * Object
    * Item of clothing, for example, headgear (related to an event, culture, religion), footwear
    * Person
    * Place
    * Event, celebration
    * Piece of music, song, lyric, dance
    * Animal, pet
D. **Important events/milestones**
    * Achievements
    * Friendships
    * Journeys (including moving schools, house, expeditions)
    * Lockdown during COVID pandemic

E. Sentence starters

★ When I was younger …

★ When I went to …

★ When I feel angry (sad, excited, frustrated etc.) …

★ I am grateful for …

★ I get angry when …

★ I am jealous of …

★ _____ makes me feel happy (sad etc.).

★ The song _____ makes me think of …

★ _____ makes me feel happy (excited, angry etc.).

★ My favourite place is …

★ When I look at the photo, I remember …

★ When I hear the song, I think of …

★ I learned an important lesson when …

Examples

What frustrates you or even makes you angry?

★ Missing clothes

★ Mislaid books or papers

★ No battery on your phone

★ A slow internet connection

★ Crowded buses

★ Traffic jams

★ Long queues

★ Being kept waiting

★ Sharing a tablet or computer

★ Sharing a bedroom

What makes you anxious?

    ★ A test

    ★ People gossiping, spreading rumours

    ★ Too much work

    ★ Owning up to a 'mistake'

    ★ Social media

What makes you nervous?

    ★ Speaking in public

    ★ A big sports match, competition or concert

What makes you excited?

    ★ A special celebration

    ★ Release of a new video game, book, album, smart phone

    ★ Going to a match, concert

    ★ Holidays

    ★ School trips

    ★ A new challenge

Questions to promote deeper thinking

1. Favourite photo: what does it show about you?
2. Favourite memory: what does it reveal about you?
3. An important time in your life: why was it important? How did it change your life?
4. Happiest time in your life: why was it the happiest?
5. Biggest challenge: what was the challenge and how did you overcome it?
6. Favourite song: what does it reveal about you?

Photographic record

Select a number of photos of:

- ★ The most important people in your life
- ★ Most treasured objects
- ★ Special collections
- ★ Favourite holidays or celebrations
- ★ Important customs or traditions

Take photos of:

- ★ Favourite recipes
- ★ Certificates

EXERCISE: FREEWRITING A MEMORY LIST

- ★ Allow **five minutes** to write any memories that instantly come to mind without taking the pen off the paper.
- ★ If you run out of ideas, just keep writing one of the sentence starters, for example, '**I remember …**,' '**I feel …**' or '**When I …**'
- ★ Do not censor what you write.
- ★ Spelling, punctuation and grammar are not important at this stage.
- ★ No need to write in full sentences – words and phrases are sufficient *memory joggers*.
- ★ When the five minutes are up, look through the list and choose one to write off.

Note: The time limit is flexible, and the list can always be revisited at another time and more memories added.

MEMORY LIST MODEL

* Bitten by Rusty the dog.
* The swivelling tap incident in the physics laboratory and soaking Katie Evans – letter home – on Mr Rogers' radar.
* My bobble hat – memories of hours standing on a rugby touchline in the freezing cold watching a game, supporting my son, my team. Wearing a branded supporters' bobble hat to declare my allegiance. Highs and lows, victories and elation, losses and disappointment – vivid memories of tries scored, tackles missed.
* Happy pink shoes worn when I feel like skipping and dancing.
* Mystery of the missing pickled onions.
* Playing crazy golf on the lawn and flicking the golf ball into the large kitchen window. Mammy thought her new pressure cooker had exploded and launched itself through the window. Ran and hid all day.
* Taking all the labels off the tin cans, and having to have a *surprise* tea, not knowing what was inside the tins that mammy chose – corned beef and pears.
* Being chased by the stallion across the field. The great stallion dare dash.
* Camping in Nana's farm with the guides and sneaking off at night to have a bath in Nana's house. Going home after two days.
* Lock on church toilet doors faulty – trapped. Lights turned off, doors locked, everyone left. Phobia of enclosed spaces.
* Walking to Nana's farm in the snow to rescue them with some milk, but not telling mammy and daddy. Search party out looking for me.
* Days out at Horton Beach.
* Holiday in Blackpool – donkeys, amusements (Nana), shows, and asthma.
* Songs – "Calon Lan" (Nana – happy heart); "Smoke Gets in Your Eyes" (smell of roast dinners and mammy singing); "The Greatest Love of All" (liking yourself).

7

External sources as writing prompts

Responding to current issues: local, national and international

Events in the news and on social media produce strong reactions and debate, so they are an excellent source for personal writing.

Where a writer has experience of the issues covered in the news, the headlines might provoke a very personal response. For example:

- ★ Experiencing racism or any form of discrimination
- ★ Bullying on social media
- ★ Social media as a lifeline to keep connected during school closures
- ★ Difficulties of learning online during school closures
- ★ Taking part in a climate change march

DOI: 10.4324/9781003215653-8

EXERCISE

Record newspaper headlines, extracts or quotes in writing journals of any events or debates that are interesting and provoke powerful emotions, or cut them out and keep them in a scrap book. For example:

* ⭐ Incidents of racism
* ⭐ The debate about the mental health effects of social media
* ⭐ Climate change
* ⭐ Closure of schools during the Covid pandemic
* ⭐ Health and fitness
* ⭐ Body image

Classes and tutor groups can create a news bulletin board that can be used for discussion and debate and a stimulus for personal writing.

Following are examples of headlines about:

1. The positive and negative impact of social media
2. Racism in sport
3. Young people striking and attending climate change marches

Note: These are just a few of the current issues; there are many more that could have been included. Decide on a current local, national and international topic and collect a variety of headlines from a range of sources for a news bulletin board and a stimulus for discussion and writing. Classes could investigate the power of communication (speech and writing) by young people to draw attention to climate change and discuss how they could use their voices to put pressure on social media companies to make their platforms safe from abuse. Apart from stimulating discussion, these are incredibly fertile areas to develop young people's interest in current affairs and to develop their powers of oracy and rhetoric.

   Note: Combined with current social and political issues, it may be of interest to apprentice writers to read about historical events such as the Candy Bar Protests in Canada in 1947 (https://en.wikipedia.org/wiki/Candy_bar_protest).

1. SOCIAL MEDIA: FRIEND OR FOE?

During the Covid pandemic of 2020, social media was a lifeline for many people, combating the isolation and loneliness caused by the restrictions on our lives. It was a place to connect and reflect, and seek help, guidance and support. However, there are also reports of young people finding it a toxic environment that has had an impact on their mental health.

The following pages include a number of headlines on this subject taken from newspapers and research findings, together with a reflection on the debate. Their aim is to act as a stimulus for discussion and personal writing: positive or negative.

EDUCATION SECRETARY TO ONLINE CELEBS: TAKE GREATER RESPONSIBILITY FOR YOUR YOUNG FOLLOWERS

The Education Secretary has today called on social media influencers and online celebrities to promote healthy body image stereotypes to the young people who follow them.

Speaking out on #StopCyberBullyingDay, Damian Hinds has called on social media influencers to help in the fight against negative body image by making sure their social media content is less appearance focused and ensuring there is more transparency about how social media photos are edited.

… 40 per cent of teenagers said that things their friends have said have made them worry about their body image …

…

Education Secretary Damian Hinds said:

"Children are growing up with a warped view of what is normal because so much of what they see on social media is false.

"These days there's a filter for everything, so much so that when something 'real' goes online it's tagged as #NoFilter but there should also be #NotEdited.

"I want social media influencers to think about what they are putting on their platform – is it honest? Is it authentic? Is it too image focused?"

Department of Education (2019)
https://www.fenews.co.uk/press-releases/31095-education-secretary-damian
-hinds-is-calling-on-social-media-influencers-to-take-
responsibility-for-their-young-audience

INSTAGRAM RANKED WORST FOR MENTAL HEALTH IN TEEN SURVEY

Summary:

★ 1,479 young people aged 14–24 took part in a survey to 'score popular social media apps on issues such as anxiety, depression, loneliness, bullying, body image and "fear of missing out" – where social media peers appear to be having a happier and more rewarding life.'

★ 'Despite many headlines about the negative effects – the report by the Royal Society for Public Health also explored the potential benefits for teenagers, such as improved sense of community and self-identity.'

★ 'YouTube was found to have the most positive impact on young people, and photo-sharing platform Instagram the most negative.'

★ 'Acting on this information, the report calls for measures to help protect individuals when using social media platforms.'

★ 'Their recommendations revolve around increased education on cyber safety and providing more help to protect mental wellbeing of young people.'

Status of Mind, Royal Society for Public Health (2017)

**SOCIAL MEDIA: POSITIVE OR NEGATIVE
INFLUENCE ON YOUNG PEOPLE?**

The report by the Prince's Trust on 5 February 2019 revealed the two sides of the social media debate. Whilst over a third of the respondents reported that when viewed through the lens of social media they felt that their lives compared negatively to those of their peers, according to the report the 'effects of social media on young people are still unclear' with over a quarter reporting that time spent on social media had a positive effect on their lives.

'Social media putting "overwhelming pressure" on
young people,' Prince's Trust (2019)

SHOULD 11- TO 12-YEAR-OLDS USE SOCIAL NETWORKING SITES?

Half of all 11- to 12-year olds have a social media profile despite the minimum age being 13. The survey by the UK Council for Child Internet Safety (UKCCIS) and the National Society for the Prevention of Cruelty to Children (NSPCC) in February 2014 reported that this has had a detrimental effect on this group of young people who have experienced trolling, exclusion from friendship groups and feelings of distress, shame, humiliation and betrayal. Some reported that they had experienced an upsetting event almost every day and nearly one-fifth were upset and even scared for weeks or months after an incident. These results raise serious questions about the responsibility of social media companies to enforce the minimum age limit of 13.

Ruth Ball and Claire Lilley, UKCCIS and NSPCC (2014)

SOCIAL MEDIA: FRIEND OR FOE?

Social media in the year 2020 was the very centre of our lives. We loved and hated it and had good reason for doing so. The people who occupied that technological space were friend and foe in equal measure. Without it, our lives may have been very different.

Social media provided us with all sorts of fascinating distractions; kept us up to date with latest trends; kept us connected to our peers; and gave us a platform to rekindle old friendships, make new friends and find new interests. It was our social staple: an essential part of our daily diet.

But it had one terrible drawback which transformed it from a centre of discovery and communication to a chamber of horrors – sometimes enabling those terrors to slither into our homes, seep through the walls and poison our 'safe spaces.'

It had the power to decide what constituted success or failure; the power to spread fake news and malicious lies; to decide whether you were in or out; to undermine and destroy. In the wrong hands, it was a venomous snake spreading its poison through the fibre optic cables hiding underground, which hummed and thrummed day and night, searching, sending, liking, tweeting, scanning, uploading: fogging our minds.

Maybe it had become a terror and a bully; a mind-manipulating software that couldn't be controlled, couldn't be regulated, and could only be stopped by cutting it off at the source. Maybe!

Alison Wilcox (2020)

2. RACISM IN SPORT: SHOW IT THE RED CARD

The terrible racism directed to players at the England v Bulgaria match in October 2019 produced nationwide uproar, and racism in sport is once again attracting news headlines, along with the marked increase in racist abuse on social media. Following is a statement from the Greater Manchester Police responding to the racist abuse experienced by Marcus Rashford and other Manchester United players, together with a powerful, inspirational response by Marcus Rashford to the racist abuse he experienced personally.

Sometimes, the feelings and thoughts resulting from a news item can be best expressed using the power of poetry. Next time an item in the news evokes strong feelings, jot down some brief thoughts and feelings and use these to write a poem. Two poems are included: *Look at the World* by Langston Hughes and *Never Surrender to Racism*, a poem I wrote in response to the anger that such abuse evoked in me personally.

The website for *Show Racism the Red Card* has a fabulous array of resources to support schools in dealing with the issue of racism (https://www.theredcard.org /education-pack). There are also links in the Appendix to sporting organisations and their stand against racism.

MARCUS RASHFORD ABUSED ON SOCIAL MEDIA

Marcus Rashford MBE, a campaigner recognised for his work demanding action on child food poverty, faced racist abuse on social media following United's 0–0 draw with Arsenal on 30 January 2021.

According to a statement that was released on Sunday, 31 January, Greater Manchester Police acknowledged that they were aware of the abuse and commented: 'Nobody should be subject to such abuse and it is deeply upsetting not only to those who suffer it, but to all those who come across this awful language too … These hateful words have no place in our society whether online or otherwise' (Greater Manchester Police, www.facebook .com/499223133910599/posts/greater-manchester-police-we-are-aware -of-a-number-of-manchester-united-football/1049552625544311/).

Responding to the racist abuse in his tweet of 31 January 2021, Marcus Rashford told his abusers that he was a proud black man, and their racism would not affect that. He refused to react to their attacks or repeat their comments. He described his followers as 'beautiful children of all colours' who should be celebrated, and whom he would not expose to the words of those who reflected 'humanity and social media at its worst' (@MarcusRashford, 31 January 2021).

I LOOK AT THE WORLD

I look at the world
From awakening eyes in a black face –
And this is what I see:
This fenced-off narrow space
Assigned to me.

I look then at the silly walls
Through dark eyes in a dark face –
And this is what I know:
That all these walls oppression builds
Will have to go!

I look at my own body
With eyes no longer blind –
And I see that my own hands can make
The world that's in my mind.
Then let us hurry, comrades,
The road to find.

By Langston Hughes (2009)

NEVER SURRENDER TO RACISM

Never surrender:
To the menace of racism:
the desolation of discrimination.

Fight it with your minds;
Fight it with your hearts;
Fight it with your voices.

Defend the right
of all our countrymen,
to equality, dignity, respect,
to play without prejudice.

Never close your ears.
Never look away.
Never accept its okay.

By Alison Wilcox (2019),
responding to the appalling racism in the
England v Bulgaria match 14 October 2019

3. ACTION FOR CLIMATE CHANGE

**FRIDAYS FOR FUTURE CAPTURES THE ATTENTION
OF THE WORLD'S MEDIA**

The Youth Climate Movement continues to grow into a global network of campaigns.

During the Global Week for Future (20–27 September 2019), millions of young people across the world joined demonstrations to demand action and secure the future of the planet they will inhabit. Possibly the largest climate strikes in world history, with more than 4 million protestors, many of whom were schoolchildren, the demonstrations captured the attention of the world's media.

ACT NOW TO SECURE THE FUTURE OF OUR PLANET

Across the globe, children abandoned their classrooms.

School children from countries across the world have taken to the streets demanding that world leaders take decisive action to tackle the climate crisis, warning those in power, 'The youth of this world has started to move, and we will not rest again.'

"Young people want and deserve a role … to make global leaders aware and act on their concerns … They have a stake in the future as this is the planet they will inherit; it is they who will bear the impact of a changing climate."

Jayathma Wickramanayake (UN Youth Envoy)
https://news.un.org/en/story/2019/09/1046882

UN SECRETARY GENERAL SUPPORTS YOUNG PROTESTORS

My generation has failed to respond properly to the dramatic challenge of climate change. This is deeply felt by young people. No wonder they are angry.

Antonio Guterres https://www.un.org/sg/en/content
/sg/articles/2019-03-15/the-climate-emergency-and-
the-next-generation

**GUTERRES HIGHLIGHTS IMPACT OF CLIMATE
CHANGE ON PACIFIC ISLANDS**

On his recent Pacific tour to the frontlines of the global climate emergency, he heard the rallying cry "Save Tuvalu; save the world," while visiting the tiny island archipelago that is battling sea level rise and coastal erosion as warming temperatures threaten the region.

https://news.un.org/en/story/2019/05/1039431

GRETA THUNBERG

When the world is deaf
by greed and by choice,
how do you change things
with only your voice?

It's hard to be noticed,
Harder to be heard,
But she stood up and spoke,
Could not be deterred.

What made them listen?
What cut through their lies?
Not the pollution
Or the fast melting ice,

Not the experts or science,
Not hunger or flood,
Not the extinctions
Our hands red with blood,

It was her steady gaze,
On our planet, alight,
Her desperate calm,
Her demand, make it right,

It's what we'll recall
Of her fight for our youth
Her luminous words,
Her courage, her truth.

By Liz Brownlee, from *Be the Change:*
Poems to Help You Save the World (2019)

THE BEAUTIFUL PLANET

Hello, hello, this is Captain Stark
from the starship Campion.
Can we land on your beautiful planet?
Early indications suggest adequate
oxygen.
It seems we have detected
all we need to set up home.
But where do you come from,
travellers?
Have you no planet of your own?

Yes, we once had a planet
just as beautiful as yours
but the lakes all turned to acid
and the seas drowned out its shores.
Trees and grasses were dying
and the air became dusty and thin.
But why was it dying, travellers?
How did this thing begin?

Gasses from our factories
killed grass and poisoned trees
and as the sun grew hotter
icecaps melted into seas.
Water swallowed up our homes
and made Earth soggy clay.
Such terrible gasses, travellers,
that they killed a world in one day?

Oh no, it took centuries
to cut down all the trees,
for all the animals to die
from the gas in our factories.
But our leaders just wouldn't listen,
it was a terrible mistake.
But what were the factories for,
travellers?
What did the factories makes?

Wonderful, useful, brilliant things,
marvellous inventions,
bigger, better and faster machines
too helpful and useful to mention.
We couldn't do without them.
No, no one could do without these.
Yet they couldn't make air
And they couldn't make trees?

Hello! Hello! Can you hear me?
Captain Stark – the – star – ship
– Campion,
May we land on your beautiful planet?
Please! Please can you help us?
We can't – hold – out – too – long …

By Sue Hardy-Dawson, from
Where Zebras Go (2017)

IT'S TIME TO ACT

The day is dawning
When global warming
Cannot be ignored.

Ice caps are melting,
Forests are burning,
Temperatures have soared.

It's time to act:
To make a pact:
To make **our** voices heard.

By Alison Wilcox and Kitty Stevenson (2019)

8

Plot outlines

There are a variety of ways of planning a narrative or creative text. Each writer is an individual and no one process fits all. It is important, therefore, to find the method that suits each apprentice writer. Following are some examples of different methods, and it is worth trying each one before deciding which method is best suited to an individual's writing process.

It is also worth noting that the detail of the planning can vary according to the form of writing. For example, with a personal narrative, the details, characters, settings and events are already well known, so a less detailed plan may be required. However, with a fictional narrative, details of the characters, settings, events, problems and resolutions may have to be developed, and a more detailed plan is often necessary. A plan of a fictional narrative is included in the Appendix, which demonstrates the difference in the initial level of detail required at the planning stage.

Whichever method is chosen, a useful first step is to retell the story and invite the audience to ask questions, which will reveal any gaps in the narrative that will need to be filled in to ensure that the text is clear and complete.

DOI: 10.4324/9781003215653-9

From personal experience, when I wrote *Jack and the Crystal Fang*, I thought I had planned out the story until I discovered (after having written most of the chapter) that I had given Jack a problem and put him in a situation I couldn't find a way to resolve. This resulted in most of the chapter being discarded and a return to the drawing board. A useful technique in this situation is to use an annotated story map, plotting the various scenes, problems and resolutions so that there is a visual picture which clearly highlights any problems before you start writing.

A *missing person's report* is an effective form of planning and writing to develop a character profile. Imagining that the character is missing necessitates a focus on key information about appearance and personality.

EXERCISE 1

Remember: a personal narrative is written in **chronological order**.

1. Write a **list of the events** as well as you can remember them.
2. Write whatever comes in your head **without censoring**. These are likely to be the **most important details**.
3. Writing a list often triggers other actions in that scene. They can be **rearranged into order later**.
4. The most important thing – **GET SOMETHING DOWN ON PAPER**.

Tip: Write on every other line. This gives you space to add more detail later.

EXERCISE 2

1. Below are two plot summaries. Highlight the essential words and phrases that reveal **WHO**, **WHAT** and **WHERE**.
2. Write a summary for each plot of fifty words or less.
3. Reduce the plot outline to twenty-five words or less.

a. Jack and the Crystal Fang **by Alison Wilcox**

The only cure for a deadly plague sweeping the country is the crystal fang of a dragon that has terrorised the countryside for many years. Until now, the location of its den on Dragon Ridge Mountain has remained a mystery. In a race against time, Jack battles through a storm to reach the top of Dragon Ridge Mountain. With Merlin to guide him, Jack enters the dragon's den and comes face to face with the monstrous beast. A story of courage and one boy's quest to fulfil a destiny foretold by legends of long ago.

b. Ruby Red **by Alison Wilcox**

You've heard of Little Red Riding Hood; now meet her cousin, Ruby Red, who makes the same journey through the forest to visit her granny. However, Ruby Red's story takes a strange turn when she also meets a wolf in the forest. In grave danger (lost in the dark forest and sick from eating poisonous berries), Ruby learns the importance of listening to her parents, keeping her promises and not judging everyone by the actions of one member of a group.

4. Try the same technique with familiar fairy tales or legends.

EXERCISE 3

1. Summarise your plot in fifty words or less. Include basic information about **WHO**, **WHAT**, **WHERE**, **WHEN**.
2. Reduce the summary to twenty-five words or less.

Challenge:

Can you reduce the summary to six words?

SIMPLE SIX-QUESTION OUTLINE TEMPLATE

When, where, who, what, why, how, result

Question	Answer
When	
Where	
Who	
What	
Why	
How did it end	
Result	

MODEL PLOT OUTLINE: *RUSTY THE DOG*

★ On way home from school.

★ Rusty, Mrs Thomas' dog, barking.

★ Went to stroke him. Bit me.

★ Screamed all the way home.

★ Mother angry and went to see Mrs Thomas.

★ Came back laughing.

★ Mrs Thomas had told her that the dog couldn't have bitten me.

★ Embarrassed – didn't want to go to school. Daddy said – laugh with them – today's news tomorrow's fish and chips papers. Teasing won't last long.

SUMMARY MODEL: *THE SWIVELLING TAP*

1. **Fifty-word plot summary:**

   A tyrant of a physics teacher, mind-numbingly boring lessons and a swivelling tap turn into a recipe for disaster with a spectacular fountain of water soaking pupils, books, equipment and causing total carnage. No longer invisible, I was well and truly on the tyrant's radar.

2. **Twenty-five-word plot summary:**

   Experimenting with a swivelling tap and causing total carnage in a physics lessons was a bad move, especially as the teacher was a tyrant.

SIMPLE SIX-QUESTION OUTLINE MODEL

When, where, who, what, why, how, result
"Rusty the Dog"

Question	Answer
When	On way home from school.
Where	At the bottom of my street.
Who	Rusty the dog.
What	Went to pat Rusty and he attacked me.
Why	He was old and temperamental.
How did it end	Discovered Rusty had no teeth so he couldn't have hurt me.
Result	Embarrassed and didn't want to go to school as everyone knew about my humiliation.

Six-word summaries of personal writing
1. Thrill of finding new horizons – Corfu
2. A dog, a bite, no teeth
3. A teacher, laboratory: a prank backfires
4. Covid lockdown, separation from parents: homesick
5. Aloof on the outside, sad inside
6. The news, negativity, anxiety, turned off
7. Social media, pros and cons: regulation?
8. Climate change: threat, evidence and action

Six-word summaries of memoir reflections
1. Still looking for the right words.
2. It's good to laugh at yourself.
3. Writing is a tool for reflection.
4. Being a captain not a clown.
5. My heart's in Wales – my home.
6. Taking risks will reap its rewards.
7. Need to accept failure to succeed.
8. Standing up, standing out, standing firm.

9

Writing a first draft

REHEARSING THE STORY ORALLY

1. Using the plot outline, tell the story to a partner, group or the class.
2. Allow the audience to ask questions about any additional information, detail, description; or how the writer felt, what they thought.

This gives the writer ideas of what to add to their plot outline before starting the first draft.

WRITING THE FIRST DRAFT

1. Write the first draft from the plot outline.
2. This is just a draft; more detail, description etc. will be added during the revision stage.

Tips

a. **Rehearse the scene:** close your eyes for a couple of minutes and picture the scene in your head.
b. 'Pour' the first draft onto the page. (Remember to include how you felt.)
c. Do not worry about revising or editing, as this could interrupt the flow of your writing. These are dealt with in later stages of the writing process.
   i. **Revision stage:** work on **detail**, **description** and **word choices**.

DOI: 10.4324/9781003215653-10

    ii. **Editing stage:** check **spelling**, **punctuation** and **grammar**; **edit sentences**.

  d. Don't worry if some **details** are a little **'fuzzy.'** Use your **imagination to fill in the gaps** or **exaggerate the action or event** to make it **more dramatic**.

  e. **Dialogue:** don't worry if you **can't remember** the **exact words spoken**. **Imagine** what the **characters** in the scene may have **said**.

Layout on page

When writing your first draft:

1. **Double space** your writing (only write on every other line) to leave enough room to edit your work.
2. Leave a **double margin** on the left-hand side. This can be used to make editing reminders. Use a double page spread of your notebook and **write on the left-hand side**. Leave the right-hand page free for revision notes and rewrites.
3. **Number your paragraphs**, so that you can tackle one paragraph at a time when revising and editing the first draft.

Opening

Launch straight into the action.

Ending

End the narrative with a brief comment about one of the following:

* Effect this event had on your life
* How it changed you
* What you learnt

Note: Some adult writers revise paragraphs, sections or scenes as they write; others, don't want to interrupt their flow and wait until the first draft is finished. With plenty of opportunities to write first drafts, apprentice writers will discover which method suits them best, which, in any event, may vary according to the type of writing.

Whilst it is helpful to deal with coaching the writing of a text as a sequential, step-by-step process, as apprentice writers become more experienced, it is important to model that writing is often a recursive process, where sometimes, for example, it is necessary to:

* ★ return to the planning stage in the middle of writing a draft to develop ideas or rethink a plot
* ★ revise a section for clarity before continuing with the draft
* ★ edit a text as errors are spotted

10

The revision process

The introduction mentioned that experienced writers do not expect their first draft to be successful. They see it as an important step in getting their ideas down onto paper, and then work on 'crafting' the writing to achieve the effect and impact for which they are aiming during the next step in the process – the revision stage.

A common error made by apprentice writers is to forget that their reader was not 'present.' Imagining writing for a specific person who was not present at the time of the incident can be helpful. (What do I need to tell my reader so that he/she has a clear picture of the setting, characters and events?)

Re-reading the text aloud or to someone else is a useful first step. It allows the writer to 're-see' the text in a new light: (i) by hearing it read aloud, and (ii) by 'seeing' it through someone else's eyes, as well as their own. This process will quickly identify those areas that are not clear or require additional detail or description.

In a community of apprentice writers, it is essential that the environment is supportive, ground rules are established and effective feedback is modelled by the adult writer. Every writer, whether it be an apprentice or a professional, is sensitive to 'criticism' of their work. It is, therefore, important to start with what worked, what was effective.

If assisting with the revision of a text takes the form of questions and suggestions, it is incredibly effective. Initially, asking questions draws the writer's attention to an area that they could think of improving but leaves the decision to the writer as to how that can be achieved. If, however, the writer asks for suggestions, some ideas are listed in the following table.

DOI: 10.4324/9781003215653-11

Revising a text collaboratively
1. Read the text aloud.
2. Highlight any words or phrases that you find powerful, curious or interesting. Identify what has been done well. Explain why it has been done well.
3. Brainstorm any questions that the text has raised.
4. Make a note of anything that is confusing.
5. Make suggestions as to how the writing could be improved – focusing on word choice and more detailed description. Identify what could be improved. Explain how it could be improved.

Asking questions and making suggestions
★ This part is interesting. Can you tell me more about this bit?
★ I'm curious about this part. What happened after …? Where was the main character?
★ I can't quite picture this part of the scene. Can you describe it in a bit more detail?
★ Do you think you could have mentioned …?
★ Are there any other words you could use instead of '…' ?
★ Could some of these sentences be linked together?
★ I found it a little difficult to follow what you were saying in this sentence because it was quite long. Would it work better if the sentence was split into two?
★ Are you writing in the past or present tense? You have used both tenses in different scenes.
★ When the action is building at the end, could you shorten some of those last few sentences to achieve a greater impact?

CAUTION

Revising the text of an apprentice writer should not be a checklist to ensure that targeted features are included, for example, fronted adverbials, relative clauses, parenthesis etc. Whether they are appropriate for the style and purpose of the text will depend on the effect, impact and flow they have on the writing. The most important elements of the text are the content, structure, organisation and language choices used to make the writing more powerful, vivid and meaningful. It is, therefore, important not to suggest over-decorating a text to meet assessment criteria, and by doing so risk losing the apprentice writer's style and voice.

The following chapters focus on the areas which apprentice writers usually need to develop:

* Close observation and attention to detail
* Pacing of the action scenes
* Description of the setting
* 'Show not tell' techniques to bring the main character to life

11

Revising action scenes

USING SLOW-MOTION TECHNIQUE TO BUILD SUSPENSE

Experimenting with the slow-motion technique is an excellent way to add more detail and suspense during the climax to the story. It basically involves making a list of every action, however small, step by step.

In the first draft of *Rusty the Dog*, the main action comprised of a compound and complex sentence, which briefly outlined the actions of the dog.

The model demonstrates how to use the 'slow-motion' technique to build suspense by including each small action.

Example A: *Rusty the Dog*

First draft

I leaned over the gate and went to pat Rusty on the head. Before I could withdraw my hand, he snarled and sank his teeth into my flesh.

DOI: 10.4324/9781003215653-12

Breaking down the action step by step

* ★ Swung my satchel off my shoulder
* ★ Edged closer to the gate
* ★ Leaned over the gate
* ★ Kept eyes fixed on Rusty
* ★ Reached out my right hand and stopped
* ★ Checked his tail was still wagging
* ★ Reached out a little further for him to sniff
* ★ Hand steady but pulse racing
* ★ Low growl from the back of his throat
* ★ Jerked my hand back
* ★ Snarled and lunged for my hand

Revised paragraph

Swinging my satchel off my shoulder, I edged closer to the gate. I leaned over the gate, keeping my eyes fixed on Rusty, watching for any sign that he was feeling bad-tempered. Slowly, I reached out my right hand, stopped for a moment, checked that his tail was still wagging. It was. I reached out a little further. Keeping my hand as steady as possible, which was not easy as my pulse was racing. I moved my hand closer for him to sniff. A low growl came from the back of his throat; I jerked my hand back. Not quick enough. Snarling, Rusty lunged.

The revised paragraph demonstrates how by describing each small action and varying the length of the sentences, the suspense gradually builds towards the climax of the scene.

Leading up to the climax, the sentences are longer and more complex. There is a gradual shift to shorter sentence parts by the use of semicolons and then, finally, to sharp, short sentences and a sentence fragment ('Not quick enough'), which has deliberately been used to emphasise the point.

Practice exercise 1: What's behind the door?

★ Imagine you are standing outside a door.

★ You are nervous about what you will find inside.

★ Think about sounds or smells coming from the room.

★ Think about each action you would take before you finally enter the room.

MODEL 1: "THE DOOR"

Original draft: He opened the door and walked into the room.

Revised draft: Grasping the metal doorknob in his right hand, Robert turned it slowly to the left. As he pushed the door inward, the hinges groaned. A blast of icy air surged towards him from inside the room, forcing Robert to take a quick step backwards – away from the door. It had only lasted a few brief seconds, but that was enough to make him doubt whether he should even have come to this part of the house. Every instinct screamed at him to turn round. Go back down the stairs.

Taking a deep breath, Robert inched towards the door. The room was dark. His eyes darted right and left. He could only make out silhouettes of furniture. Nothing else. He pushed the door open a little further. Tentatively, he moved his right foot into the room. Then, his left foot. The floorboards creaked as they took his weight.

Practice exercise 2: What's outside the house?

* Imagine you hear an unusual noise outside your house.

* You want to look out of the window, but you don't want to be seen.

* Think about how you would move across your room and, finally, look out the window.

MODEL 2: "OUTSIDE THE HOUSE"

Original draft: She went to the window and looked out.

Revised draft: Crouching on all fours, Kitty manoeuvred around the bedroom towards the window. Slowly, she lifted her head above the sill. A beam of light swung across the front of the house. Kitty threw herself to the floor. She waited a moment until the beam had disappeared, and then, slowly, levered herself up. The glare of the beam was focused on next door's house. She crouched behind the curtain for a few more seconds. Then, inching the curtain back a few centimetres, she lifted her head above the sill. She peered out. Kitty knew she would never forget what she saw through that window.

Example B: *The Incident of the Swivelling Tap*

First draft

As Mr Rogers turned his back, I turned the tap. A fountain of water shot into the air and soaked everyone on the bench in front.

Breaking down the action step by step

* Mr Rogers chalking diagram on the board – screeching chalk
* Back turned to the class
* Kept an eye on Mr Rogers
* Slid fingers towards the tap
* Twisted it until the spout faced the ceiling
* Mr Rogers whipped around
* Scanned the class
* Held my breath
* Stared at my exercise book
* Prayed he hadn't noticed I wasn't holding my pencil
* Mr Rogers turned back to the board
* Beverley mouthed: "Go on. Turn it on"
* Kathryn shook her head; moved her seat away from mine
* Swivelled the tap, turned it on
* Carnage – spectacular fountain of water
* Crashed into the ceiling
* Curved downwards
* Dropped heavy load on to the head of Katie Evans
* Bench soaked, exercise books soaked, textbooks, pencil cases – all sodden
* Everyone leapt to feet
* Grabbed books and pencil cases
* Watched water pour from the bench and formed a puddle on the floor

Revised paragraph

Mr Rogers was busy chalking another diagram on the board, the chalk screeching as he labelled the various parts. His back was turned. Keeping my eye on Mr Rogers, I slid my fingers towards the tap and twisted it until the spout faced the ceiling. He seemed to have an instinct for anyone not studiously working in his lesson and at the slightest noise he would whip round, his fierce blue eyes scanning the class. I held my breath and looked intently at my exercise book, praying that he didn't notice that I wasn't holding my pencil. His eyes narrowed for a moment, and then he turned his back and continued with his diagram.

Everyone on my bench was watching excitedly to see what I would do next. Most were grinning, anticipatory. Would the tap still work? What would happen if it did? I glanced at Beverley, who was grinning from ear to ear and mouthed to me, "Go on. Turn it on."

Kathryn stared at me in horror and shook her head, her eyes wide with panic. She knew I never could resist a dare. When she realised that I was ignoring her, Kathryn edged her seat further away from mine. She didn't want to have anything to do with this prank.

Never in my wildest dreams could I have imagined the carnage that followed. I wasn't even convinced that the tap could work upside down. I thought at best there would be a trickle of water, possibly onto the floor. Never did I foresee such a spectacular fountain of water spurting out of that tap, crashing into the ceiling and curving downwards to drop its heavy load on to the head of Katie Evans and the bench directly in front. The bench was soaked, exercise books, textbooks, pencil cases all sodden. Everyone on the front bench had leapt to their feet, screaming, grabbing their books and pencil cases, watching as the water poured from the bench to collect in puddles on the laboratory floor.

12

Setting

In personal writing, there are occasions where the setting is the key element of the text, for example, *First Morning in Corfu* and *Rwy'n Gartref*. On other occasions, it is a backdrop to the main characters and the events, for example, the science laboratory in *The Swivelling Tap Incident* or the hospital in *Discovering a Writing Journal*. Whether describing settings or characters, the following poem describes how observation and recording the sights, sounds or smells, touch, taste, or feelings in a notebook is the key ingredient to powerful, memorable writing.

EXERCISE

Use the model of the "Spider's Web" table, which follows the poem "Word Pictures", to practise describing interesting objects by asking a series of questions.

DOI: 10.4324/9781003215653-13

WORD PICTURES

Stand still for a moment.
Open your eyes wide:
Watch, observe, look closely, zoom in.
Be curious about what you see.
Take another look.
Take a picture in your mind.
Write what you see, what you feel.
Write what you hear, what you smell.
Write what you touch or taste.
Record the moment, the image.
Store the seed in your notebook.
Take it out, water it.
Give it air, give it light.
It will develop and grow,
into a picture in words.

By Alison Wilcox (2019)

DESCRIBING AN OBJECT, SCENE, LANDSCAPE

This is a picture of a spider's web in the grass early one morning. Taking a picture allows the writer to zoom in and focus on small details, to capture the moment to study later.

Ask the following questions	
Name each part of the picture.	Web, strands, blades of grass, drops, pearls, dew, breeze
What does it look like?	A piece of lace
What adjective(s) can I use to describe it?	Silvery, shimmering, delicate
What is it doing?	Blowing, shimmering, shivering in the breeze
Delicate, silver strands of shimmering lace shivering between thick blades of grass.	

Writers take time to observe people, places, things. They pay close attention to their surroundings to sharpen their observation skills and practise focusing on the small details: the things that most people miss, including using all their senses – sight, sound, smell, touch and taste. Close observations make writing sharp, clear, vivid and help bring descriptions to life.

EXERCISE: OBSERVATION PRACTICE	
Imagine you are standing outside your house, school, a favourite place, and answer the following questions.	
What do you see? Look for the small details.	
What do you hear? Smell? Touch?	
What is the weather like?	

(Also see "Scene/image box plan template" and "Scene/image box plan model" in the Appendix.)

EXERCISE: AN IMPORTANT PERSONAL SETTING

* Draw a labelled map of the route and the setting to help you.
* Make a note of scenery, buildings, landmarks etc.
* Describe the setting using the following:
  To the right, to the left, in front, behind, above, below, in the distance.
* Zoom in on your destination.
* Use similes from normal, everyday sights or objects to help your reader visualise the scene.
* Move through the building and describe what you see.
* Open a door and describe what is in the room using:
  Size, shape, furniture, objects, pictures etc.
  Use: in the middle, on the floor, against the wall, by the window etc.
* What can you hear and smell?
* What do you touch? What does it remind you of?
* How does the scene make you feel?
  Scaffolding: To help you, use the sentence stem: 'I take a mental picture of this scene so that I will always remember …'

FIRST DRAFT

I was so excited. It was Nana's birthday, and everyone was going to meet up at the farm. When we got there, everyone was already crowded into the kitchen.

MODEL TEXT

1. Using the following revised text, highlight useful words or phrases that 'move' the reader through the setting.
2. Highlight the words and phrases that describe other senses (sound, smell).

REVISED TEXT: A FAMILIAR SETTING

As we travel along the main road to the coast, the marsh spreads out before us on the right. The tide is out, so groups of wild ponies are visible, scattered over the marsh. The shriek of a seagull drifts in through the window. We are nearing the coast.

Suddenly, I see it: a steep, winding road off to the left up into the hills. It is usually narrow, but in the height of summer, the hedges are bursting with growth and arching over the road, making it little more than a track. We go slowly and pause at every sharp bend to make sure there is no car coming down the hill. A sudden scratching sound alerts us to a stray sharp twig sticking out of the hedge and scraping against the side of the car.

After a few miles, the road narrows and we turn down a rutted track overlooking the green fields, with the hills in the distance shielding the coast. The rutted track throws us from side to side as the car suddenly leaps into the air. Within a mile, we arrive at the large, five-bar white gate across the track, which leads into the farmyard.

I leap out, pull back the lever, edge the gate open and wait for the car to go through. As I wait, I scan the fields for the horses, then spot the pigpen over to my right. Making sure that the gate is firmly closed, I leap excitedly back into the car. Not far now. I can see the farmhouse just visible as we follow the track round to the left: past the pigs snuffling in their pen; past the cow sheds on the right, doors slightly ajar letting the stench of manure waft towards us.

We pull up in the large square on the right-hand side of the farmhouse. Several cars are parked there. The others have already arrived.

As I leave the car, the distinctive tickle in my nose alerts me to the deadly pollen drifting towards me from the barn opposite. Bales of hay stacked high to the ceiling are visible through the open doors. I quickly head indoors.

In front of us is the two-storey stone farmhouse, with its heavy wooden front door firmly shut; it is only ever opened to special visitors, who are led into the parlour.

We make our way round the back via the path down the side of the house. In front of us is the vegetable patch, with rows of tripods like tepees covered in green beans; lines of huge cabbages like something out of *The Day of the Triffids*, and in the corner, the dreaded rhubarb patch, the thick pink sticks and enormous crinkled leaves mocking me from a distance. I take a moment to offer up a prayer that rhubarb tart is not on the menu today.

Eventually, we arrive at the old, oak stable door. As usual, the top half is wide open. Leaning over, I lift the latch and step inside. The cold, stone flagstones are scrubbed and gleaming in the sunlight.

Further down the passage, is another wooden door leading to the lounge. All along the passage are family photos, some ancient, others displaying brand new members of the clan.

A cheer erupts from the television: must be a rugby match. As we enter the lounge, I spot the familiar huge hearth to my right – logs stacked in a pile even in summer.

I smile at the familiar, comforting sight of the two old comfy armchairs side by side: the imprint of their recent inhabitants still visible in the cushions. A large well-worn sofa stands against the wall opposite the window looking out onto the farmyard. Brass ornaments are lined up and gleaming in an alcove to the left of the fireplace. Family photos are displayed on the shelves to the right. The room is strangely empty.

Raucous laughter explodes from behind the door; they are all in the kitchen. Now I can smell baking – fresh bread and biscuits – wafting from the kitchen. As the door opens, I catch sight of a sea of bodies; everyone crowded round the huge kitchen table; everyone talking in loud excited voices and all talking at once.

There are loaves of fresh bread on a huge wooden table. Some members of the family are seated at the tables shelling peas, others buttering mounds of bread, cutting cakes, putting them on plates, pouring tea into the numerous cups. As normal, everyone has their job.

I catch a glimpse of Nana through the open pantry door and spot the stone shelves lined with jars, tins, preserves, huge bags of flour and an enormous urn of fresh milk. I take a mental picture of this scene, so that I will always remember the familiar, comforting sights, sounds, smells and warm embrace of a large family.

I WOULD REALLY LIKE TO GO BACK TO ...

... CORFU

Remembering a favourite place, particularly now travel is restricted, is a great way of escaping the gloomy wet days of winter. Following is a copy of notes from a writing journal, together with a typed version to demonstrate the writing process and the value of having a notebook to jot down ideas, feelings, sights and sounds as you experience them.

Only words and phrases have been jotted down of the sunrise and the sounds of early morning in Corfu to capture the details for a future description or narrative.

These notes are used to write a first draft, which is then revised a number of times: adding and substituting words and phrases; changing the order and length of the sentences until it accurately reflects the sights and sounds of that moment.

Tip: Get a writers' notebook so you can jot down things that you see and how you feel – capture the moment. It's a wonderful record to help you recall the memory and helps to develop your writing.

EXERCISE

Read *First Morning in Corfu*.

Highlight any words or phrases that you think are powerful and descriptive.

Make a note of the senses used: sights, sounds, touch.

Sept. 2019

Cockerel choir calling

Echoes across the valley
Greeting – welcome – alarm call

One eye closed – sluggish

crawl out of bed. Wow < run for notebook pen
Watch – entranced
sun peaks
thin wispy strands of peach

Spread, thicken
bands
Mysterious mist
Albanian hills – veil
Sun rises tears, gaps tiny
balls of
Crystalline shimmer - light

like fairy lights

Page 1 of notebook

Cockerel choir calling – echoes – across the valley

Greeting – welcome – alarm call

One-eye closed, sluggish – half-awake – crawl out of bed

Wow! Run for notebook and pen

Watch – entranced

Sun peeks over horizon

Thin wispy strands of peach

Spreads, thickens – bands

Mysterious mist shrouds Albanian hills – veil

Sun rises – tears, gaps in veil

Tiny balls of light

Crystalline shimmer

Like fairy lights

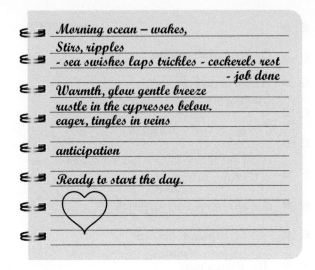

Page 2 of notebook

Morning ocean – wakes

Stirs, ripples

Sea swishes, laps, trickles

Cockerels rest – job done

Warmth, glow – gentle breeze

Rustle in the cypresses below

Eager, tingle in veins

Anticipation

Ready to start the day

Alison Wilcox (September 2019, Notebook)

FIRST MORNING IN CORFU

The cockerel choir has started up, crowing, "Get up. Open your windows. Come and see the dawn." They are loud, persistent, their echoes rebounding across the valley.

Slowly, sluggishly, one eye half-closed, I crawl out of bed and make my way to the balcony, murmuring under my breath about being woken up so early on the first day of my holiday.

Standing on the balcony, I am immediately entranced by the scene. The sun is just peeking over the horizon and painting thin, wispy strands of peach across the sky. Gradually, the bands thicken and spread as the sun rises. In the distance, the mysterious shadow of the Albanian hills is just visible, shrouded by a layer of mist. Then, as if dawn has exploded, it fills the sky with its blazing bright orange light.

As the sun continues to rise, the cockerels go quiet. The morning sea begins to stir. A crystalline shimmer spreads across its surface as if nature's fairy lights have suddenly been turned on. A gentle breeze springs up and rustles in the huge cypress trees below, then ripples across the surface of the sea, sending waves to swish and slosh onto the beach.

What a glorious welcome to Corfu. There is a glow, a warmth, an anticipation tingling in my veins. I'm ready to start the day.

Model of a setting outline using sensory description and emotions

FIRST DRAFT

My favourite place is the beach. I've really missed the sight and sounds of home: the beaches and the sea, which carry many happy and familiar memories.

PLANNING

My favourite place is: the beach

Reminds me of: home

Sights: cove, craggy cliffs; steep winding path; huge boulders; sun dappled golden sand, brilliant blue sky; waves curling at my feet; scattered shells on the water's edge; foaming spray of the waves; swirling, dancing around my legs

Touch: feel of the warm sand between my toes; wind tugging my hair; icy water sloshing against my legs

Smell: salty smell of the ocean, seaweed

Feelings: freedom from the noise and bustle; calm, comforting, **HOME!**

Thoughts: lots of memories of playing on the beach and swimming in the sea as a child

---

Using a setting brainstorm to craft a poem

Poetry is a good way to develop a vivid setting description. As there is not a large amount of text to work with, instead focusing on the most descriptive words and phrases, it encourages experimentation with word choice and order. The poem can then be used to write an extended description of a setting to be included in a personal narrative.

Tip: For descriptive words and phrases for settings, *Descriptosaurus* provides a wide variety of choices that can be used and adapted to suit individual settings.

Rwy'n Gartref [I'm Home] is a poem written about a childhood home in Wales, which was then developed into a setting description for a personal narrative.

Rwy'n Gartref

At the beach, I am free:
free from the noise, the bustle.
I throw off my shoes,
feel the sun dappled sand between my toes.
Stand and breathe deeply.
Listen to the waves crashing against the cliffs.

Shells tossed by the tide,
scattered treasures of years gone by
lead me to the water's edge.
I close my eyes, inhale deeply:
savour those memories.

I rejoice at the salty smell of the ocean spray:
dancing, swirling, sloshing around my legs.
The wind tugs my hair from its band
to dance wildly.

I can hear children laughing,
splashing in the shallows,
sending water over the shivering shilly-shalliers.
Calling to one another,
plunging through the waves
into the icy cold surf.

Memories wrap around me like an old blanket.
Rwy'n gartref. I am home.

By Alison Wilcox (2019)

Rwy'n Gartref

It feels good to be back after all this time. For the first time in months, I feel free. The precarious scramble down the steep winding path has been worth the effort, and I have chosen a great day to revisit old memories. Not much has changed. Steep, craggy cliffs surround the cove on all sides. The only difference is the pile of huge boulders that nestle at the base of the south cliff, evidence of the tragic cliff collapse decades ago. The small, sheltered cove is deserted now, not like in the past.

Today, the sun blazes from a brilliant blue sky over a sea that shimmers as if crystals have been sprinkled between the ripples: its warmth wrapping round my body like a fleecy blanket.

I throw off my shoes, feel the sun dappled sand between my toes. For a moment, I stand still and listen to the waves crashing against the cliffs.

Shells tossed by the tide, scattered treasures of years gone by, lead me to the water's edge. I close my eyes, inhale deeply and savour those memories. I rejoice at the salty smell of the ocean spray that is curling and lapping at my feet. The wind tugs my hair from its band, sending it dancing wildly in the breeze. As I stand there, I can hear children laughing, splashing in the shallows and sending water over the shivering shilly-shalliers. They call to one another and I can see them plunging through the waves into the cold depths. That was a long time ago. Now when a wave surges onto the beach and breaks into circles of dancing water to soak the bottom of my trousers, it sends me scampering back onto dry land.

Today, except for the soothing swish, splash and slosh of the waves, there is no other sound. No birds singing. No voices of excited children playing on the beach.

As I walk back to the cliffs, I wriggle my toes so that the golden sand trickles over my feet. I feel like the only person on earth as I wrap those memories around me like an old, comforting blanket. Rwy'n gartref. I am home.

By Alison Wilcox (2021)

SETTING AS PART OF A PERSONAL NARRATIVE

As shown below, brainstorm the setting by making a list of the objects that are in the room.

SETTING OUTLINE MODEL: THE SCIENCE LAB

* Four rows of long, wooden benches; high wooden, uncomfortable stools
* Sinks and gas taps; steel cabinet
* Glass cases full of trays of test tubes, chemicals, wires, batteries, plugs and bulbs
* All very exciting but locked away and out of bounds – never to be touched by the pupils
* White, sterile, freshly painted walls
* Teacher's desk: huge wooden bench, covered in trays, spilling wire and tubes and all sorts of paraphernalia, tub of different coloured chalks, huge wooden ruler, two board rubbers, stacks of exercise books
* Enormous blackboard – spidery writing and complicated diagrams
* Sunny outside – feeling of gloom inside the lab

TIP: USING WEATHER TO REFLECT A MOOD

Think about how you were feeling at this setting. Weather and seasons are a great way of reflecting your mood or the atmosphere in the setting.

For example, a bright, sunny day for a happy memory; wind for a scary event; dark skies and rain for an unhappy event.

On the other hand, you can contrast the weather outside with the atmosphere inside the setting. For example, 'Outside the sun was shining on the playing fields, but inside there was an atmosphere of gloom.'

> **TIP: EXPANDING DESCRIPTION OF THE WEATHER OR LIGHT AT THE SETTING TO BUILD AN ATMOSPHERE/SUSPENSE**
>
> **First draft**
>
> It was dark.
>
> **Revised text**
>
> The light faded and then the night slowly drew a black cloak across the sky and sent the darkness slithering into every space around me, spreading across the ceiling, down the walls and across the floor as I waited for the sound of their car on the drive. It was an unsettling darkness, full of dancing shadows and the occasional creak and rustle from the house.

First draft

We entered the science laboratory quietly and hurried to our seats.

Revised text: The science laboratory

When we entered the science lab, we always lingered, stopped for a brief moment, glanced longingly at the glass cabinets full of test tubes and glass jars full of brightly coloured chemicals, and trays of wires and tubes, bulbs and batteries and lots of other fascinating equipment that we knew we would never get to touch.

Outside the sun was shining on the playing fields, but inside there was an atmosphere of gloom. We slunk towards one of the long wooden benches and hurriedly took our seats as Mr Rogers stomped into the room. He marched over to his enormous wooden desk, which was covered in trays spilling wire and tubes and all sorts of paraphernalia: a tub of different coloured chalks, a huge wooden ruler, two board rubbers (one for use on the blackboard, the other as a missile to attract the attention of anyone not listening), stacks and stacks of exercise books awaiting his red pen. Behind him was his favourite piece of equipment: an enormous blackboard covered in his spidery writing and complicated diagrams.

Zooming in on the setting to build a vivid picture and atmosphere
Example: *Discovering a Writing Journal*

First draft
I followed my father through the entrance to the hospital and down a number of corridors before he stopped suddenly outside a room and vanished inside.

Zooming in on the setting using senses: sight, sound, touch, smell
Walls were stark, white, cold.
Floor tiles were white, cold, shiny, sterile – my shoes squeaked.
Smell of disinfectant, overwhelming – clogged nostrils.
Nurses marched past, in and out of swing doors.
Starched uniforms rustled as they walked.
Metal trays with gleaming instruments rattled.
Smell of chicken stew – tea-time.
In the distance, trolley creaked, and cups rattled.

Revised text: *Discovering a Writing Journal*

As we made our way to the entrance of the hospital, through the swinging doors and into the building, Daddy seemed to have forgotten I was there. With his enormous strides, he marched purposefully through the building towards the stairs. Even though I was sweating from the effort of trying to keep up with him, I felt cold. The walls were stark, white and cold. The floor tiles were also white, and cold, shiny and sterile. I remember my shoes squeaking on the tiles.

   The first thing I noticed when we entered the building was the smell of disinfectant, and as we climbed the stairs, the smell became overwhelming, seeping into the back of my throat and clogging my nostrils.

   Nurses marched past me, up and down the corridor, and out of numerous swing doors: their starched uniforms rustling as they walked; their metal trays, with their gleaming instruments rattling ominously. As one of the doors behind me swung open, the stench of disinfectant faded to be replaced by the smell of chicken stew. In the distance, a trolley creaked, and cups rattled.

13

Characters

Developing good observation skills is an important part of improving your writing. Great writers observe their surroundings carefully and are keen people-watchers.

EXERCISE: SCHOOL OR HOME

Watch someone close to you very carefully when they are, for example, completing a task, doing maths problems, watching a sporting fixture, driving a car, reacting to a situation.

Make a list of their actions, movements, facial expressions. Pay attention to anything that is peculiar to them. Show the description to one of your friends or family and see if they can guess who you are describing.

There are a variety of ways to develop a character description:

(a) Brainstorm a list of physical features, character traits and actions.
(b) Use a picture of a person or pet and imagine what that character was saying. An example is included later in *Alfie Misses Out on a Piece of Bacon*.
(c) Character investigations: Develop a list of interview questions to gain more information about the character. It is an ideal way to break down the 'show not tell' technique, which many apprentice writers find so difficult to grasp.

DOI: 10.4324/9781003215653-14

EXERCISE: CHARACTER BRAINSTORMING

Brainstorm words and phrases for:

★ Physical description
★ Personality traits (actions that reflect personality)
★ Any distinguishing features or actions

Just write whatever comes into your head without censoring. These details are likely to be the most important. You can always add more detail later.

Note: It is not necessary and usually counter-productive to use descriptions for every single category. Pick out the main features and emphasise those. Too many details will result in the key elements being absorbed into a lengthy description and the effect will be lost.

CHARACTER CHECKLIST

★ Height/shape
★ Eyes/eyebrows
★ Skin/scars
★ Hair/facial hair
★ Mouth/lips/teeth
★ Hands/nails
★ Smell
★ Movement
★ Voice
★ Any strange habits/mannerisms
★ Behaviour

Brainstorm words and phrases for physical description and personality traits (actions that reflect these).

* Small and stocky
* Terrier
* Red and brown wiry, curly coat
* Curly mane tinted grey
* Small pointy ears like a fox
* Long, thin tail curled like a scorpion
* Chubby, little legs
* Small, dark, beady eyes
* Small, puckered mouth – looked disapproving
* Silvery string of slimy drool in the corner of his mouth
* Sometimes looked really pleased to see you, wagging tail furiously, balancing on hind legs and peering over the iron gate
* Yappy and bad-tempered
* Bounced on all four legs behind the gate
* Launched himself at the gate, yapping furiously
* Menacing low growl at the back of his throat
* Hairs on neck stiff like a wire brush

Tips

1. For descriptive words and phrases for characters, *Descriptosaurus* provides a wide variety of choices that can be used and adapted to suit individual settings.
2. Use photos to stimulate ideas and vocabulary, either personal photos or those found on the internet.

USING A PHOTO AND DIALOGUE: *ALFIE MISSES OUT ON A PIECE OF BACON*

You CANNOT be serious!
What sort of human are you?
I've given you the big brown doggy eyes.
I've panted loudly, with my tongue lolling out.
I've put my paw on your leg to give you a nudge.
I've put my head in your lap.
I've drooled on your trousers.
(Maybe that wasn't such a good idea!)
I CANNOT believe you still did it.
How could you?
Put that last piece of bacon into YOUR mouth?

By Alison Wilcox (2019)

Using questions to develop character descriptions

Using an investigative approach to reading texts by developing their own lists of questions, not only improves apprentice writers' understanding of the texts read, but also creates an atmosphere where curiosity is valued. Apprentice writers become engaged and enthusiastic 'detectives.' This leads to a significant improvement in their ability to infer at a deeper level as well as greatly enhancing their prediction skills. Most children's books don't directly 'tell' the reader what the character is like: the information is spread throughout the text. Apprentice writers need to learn to collect not only information about the character's appearance but, more importantly, clues about their personality type, background and experiences. They need to develop questions to discover how the character is feeling, acts, speaks and thinks: F.A.S.T. (Feelings, Actions, Speech, Thoughts).

Developing a list of meaningful questions is also an invaluable resource and an essential ability for giving apprentice writers a strategy and toolkit for revising their own work or reviewing that of their peers.

How many times has an apprentice writer's text had a comment to add more detail or description? How often has that led to them merely adding a couple of extra words? This is because they have little understanding of what has been asked of them, and often the sentences become worse after the alteration or addition.

Initially, the questions are at a basic level, mainly concerning appearance, but with practice, and some model questions to refer to, apprentice writers soon become more adept at asking more sophisticated questions in relation to personality, feelings, background and experiences of a character.

Character prompt cards are a great warm-up activity to develop this questioning approach. Each of the cards has a sentence and a series of questions to help develop an image of a character. Once pupils are familiar with the types of questions being used, they will be able to develop their own list of questions.

This approach can be used with a class, group or an apprentice writer's own text, where they develop their own prompt cards and lists of questions.

(An example of a character prompt card is included in the Appendix.)

DEVELOPING THE SKILL OF 'SHOW NOT TELL': *RUSTY THE DOG*

Write a telling sentence. For example:
I was nervous of Mrs Thomas' dog.

Rusty the dog: A 'telling' sentence

I was **nervous** of Mrs Thomas' **dog**.

(Which word(s) would you like to know more about?)
Develop a list of questions.
For example: What was his name? What did he look like? Why did he make me nervous?

I was **nervous** of Mrs Thomas' **dog**.

He was **yappy** and **temperamental**. He was a **terrier called Rusty**.

Sometimes, he looked really pleased to see you. He would run up to the gate with his tail wagging furiously, then would balance on his hind legs and peer over the gate to greet you. Other times, he would launch himself at the gate, yapping furiously.

Rusty was a small, stocky terrier, with a red and brown curly coat, small, dark, beady eyes and large pointy ears like a fox. The most peculiar thing about Rusty was his mouth. It was surrounded by grey, wiry hairs and was permanently puckered, making him look as if he disapproved of everything around him. A silvery string of slimy drool seemed to hang constantly from the left-hand corner of his mouth.

Rusty the dog: 'showing' sentences

I was nervous of Mrs Thomas' dog. His name was Rusty, and he was yappy and temperamental. He was a small, stocky terrier, with a red and brown coat, small, dark, beady eyes and pointy ears like a fox. The most peculiar thing about Rusty was his mouth. It was surrounded by wiry, grey hairs and was permanently puckered as if he disapproved of everything and everyone. A silvery string of slimy drool hung from the left-hand corner of his mouth. Sometimes, Rusty looked really pleased to see you. He would run up to the metal gate at the end of his drive, with his tail wagging furiously, then would balance on his hind legs and peer over the gate to greet you. Other times, he would launch himself at the gate, yapping furiously, the hairs on his back stiff like a wire brush.

FIRST DRAFT

I was walking home from school, swinging my satchel, eyes fixed on the pavement, deep in thought about a difficult day at school. A sudden barking broke my train of thought, and I glanced up. Mrs Thomas' dog, Rusty the terrier was at the gate, balanced on his hind legs, with his front legs gripping the top of the iron gate.

Second draft: adding more description of Rusty

Walking home, swinging my satchel, eyes fixed on the pavement, I was deep in thought about a difficult day at school. A sudden barking made me glance up. Mrs Thomas' dog was at the gate, balanced on his hind legs, with his front legs gripping the top of the iron gate, wagging his tail madly.

I was nervous of Mrs Thomas' dog. His name was Rusty, and he was yappy and temperamental. He was a small, stocky terrier, with a red and brown curly coat, small dark beady eyes and pointy ears like a fox. The most peculiar thing about Rusty was his mouth. It was surrounded by wiry, grey hairs and was permanently puckered as if he disapproved of everything and everyone. A silvery string of slimy drool hung from the left-hand corner of his mouth. Sometimes, Rusty looked really pleased to see you, like today. Other times, he would launch himself at the gate, yapping furiously, the hairs on his back stiff like a wire brush.

EXERCISE

1. Write a telling sentence about your character, including how that character made you feel. For example:
   * I loved …
   * I hated …
   * I was jealous of …
   * … made me feel …

2. With a partner or group, develop some questions to uncover additional information about your character. For example:
   * Why did you hate … ?
   * Why did you love … ?
   * What did he/she do?
   * What does he/she look like?

INNOVATING A CHARACTER DESCRIPTION

When learning how to write good character descriptions, it is sometimes useful to take a model from a published author known for their characterisation, for example, Roald Dahl, and innovate the model for your own characters. This technique is modelled in the description of Mr Rogers, which is based on Roald Dahl's character Mrs Pratchett.

BRAINSTORMING A CHARACTER OUTLINE

Model: Mr Rogers – menacing bully

★ Tall, pot-belly
★ Red face, bulging purple veins in cheeks and nose
★ White hair
★ Bushy eyebrows that meet in the middle
★ Bristly hairs protruding from nose and ears
★ Sweaty armpits
★ Tight shirt – sweat patches on stomach
★ Enormous, shovel-like hands
★ Long nails
★ Cracked knuckles
★ Smelt of stale sweat and garlic
★ Booming voice – bellowed insults – called us thick, stupid, lazy
★ Marched around the room, leant over bench with both hands on desk – fixed with piercing stare
★ Threw board rubber
★ Used ruler to strike knuckles and palms
★ Pulled up by ears

DEVELOPING THE SKILL OF 'SHOW NOT TELL': *MR ROGERS*

Mr Rogers: a 'telling' sentence

I **hated** the **physics teacher**.

(Which word(s) would you like to know more about?)

Develop a list of questions.

For example: What was his name? What did he look like? Why did you hate him?

I **hated** the **physics teacher**..

He was a **terror** and **a bully**.

His name was **Mr Rogers**.

> He used to flex his fingers and crack his knuckles menacingly as he prepared to cuff one of us round the head.

> He was a tall, pot-bellied, red-faced old brute. He had white, bristly hairs that stuck out of his ears and waggled from his nose when he shouted.

Mr Rogers: 'showing' sentences

> I hated the physics teacher. His name was Mr Rogers and he was a terror and a bully. He was a tall, pot-bellied, red-faced old brute, with white, bristly hairs that stuck out of his ears and waggled from his nose when he shouted. Before every physics lesson, I had a sick feeling in the pit of my stomach, dreading the moment he would start to flex his fingers and crack his knuckles menacingly as he prepared to cuff one of us around the head, hoping that today it would not be my turn.

Innovated description using Mrs Pratchett in Roald Dahl's book *Boy: Tales of Childhood*

The physics lab in the year 1977 was the very centre of our torture. To us it was what the Tower of London was to treasonous dukes and earls, or the ducking chair was to a witch. Without it, our lives would have been carefree. The lab was state-of-the-art, equipped with all sorts of interesting equipment, potions and powders. But it had one terrible drawback, which transformed it from a centre of discovery to a chamber of horrors. The teacher who occupied it was a terror and a bully. We hated him and we had good reason for doing so.

His name was Mr Rogers. He was a tall, pot-bellied, red-faced old bully with bristly hairs that stuck out of his ears and waggled from his nose when he shouted. He had a mouth as sour as a rhubarb tart. He always scowled. He never welcomed us when we entered the class, and the only times he spoke to us direct was to shout things like, "Are you listening?" or "Are you thick, girl?" or "Stop talking, girl and you might be able to get some of the questions right for a change."

But the most loathsome thing about Mr Rogers was the sweat that clung to him. Underneath his arms were damp and stained. His shirt was creased and stuck to his stomach and chest in crinkled patches. It erupted from his pores like the fury he vented on us, beading his upper lip and his forehead, trickling down to settle in his bushy eyebrows that met in the middle and stuck out fiercely at odd angles.

It was his hands, however, that disturbed us most: his enormous shovel-like hands, with nails like jagged claws. They were lethal. They were forever gripping some weapon – be it ruler or blackboard rubber. And do not forget please that it was those hands and fingers that were meant to be used to educate us in the wonders of science, not the pain from the thwack of a ruler. When he straightened his fingers to prepare for a blow, you couldn't help noticing the knuckles. They were misshapen as if he had been a bare-knuckle fighter in his youth and cracked like a pistol shot as he cuffed one of us around the head. There were few precious laws to protect kids in those days, and nobody, least of all me, ever thought of telling our parents or another teacher of our daily torment.

The very sight of his face reddening with fury, the purple veins bulging in his cheeks when only the front benches had understood a word of what he had said, bent our heads and fixed our eyes to the desk. We simply watched in sullen silence as yet another one of us was hit on the knuckles with a ruler for being unable to answer a question.

By Alison Wilcox (2019)

SECOND DRAFT: *DISCOVERING A WRITING JOURNAL*

In the first draft, the setting was described in more detail using a number of senses, but there was little description of the character's actions and reactions.

As we made our way to the entrance of the hospital, through the swinging doors and into the building, Daddy seemed to have forgotten I was there. With his enormous strides, he marched purposefully through the building towards the stairs. The walls were stark, white and cold. The floor tiles were also white, and cold, shiny and sterile. I remember my shoes squeaking on the tiles.

The first thing I noticed when we entered the building was the smell of disinfectant, and as we climbed the stairs, the smell became overwhelming, seeping into the back of my throat and clogging my nostrils.

Nurses marched past me, up and down the corridor, and out of numerous swing doors: their starched uniforms rustling as they walked; their metal trays, with their gleaming instruments rattling ominously. As one of the doors behind me swung open, the stench of disinfectant faded to be replaced by the smell of chicken stew.

I watched as my father turned into a room at the end of the corridor. Briefly, he looked back, gave me a quick nod, then turned and vanished into the room.

In the distance, a trolley creaked, and cups rattled.

Using actions to create a vivid picture of the character's emotions **Example:** *Discovering a Writing Journal*
In the second draft, there is little description of the character's actions and reactions. The additions to the second draft which reflect the character's emotions are shown in bold.
How did the character feel? What did the character do? How did they move?

★ Felt cold
★ Found it hard to breathe
★ Hard lump at the back of my throat
★ Desperate to see mammy, but terrified of what I would see
★ Felt as if I was invisible
★ It was tea-time, but for once I wasn't hungry
★ For the first time I saw daddy hesitate, his shoulders stooped
★ Stood rooted to the spot, taking quick, shuddering breaths
★ Sounds were muffled and distant as if I was underwater
★ Jolted into action when a door slammed behind me
★ Started to move robotically, focused on the open door

Revised paragraph

As we made our way to the entrance of the hospital, through the swinging doors and into the building, Daddy seemed to have forgotten I was there. With his enormous strides, he marched purposefully through the building towards the stairs. **Even though I was sweating from the effort of trying to keep up with him, I felt cold.** The walls were stark, white and cold. The floor tiles were also white, and cold, shiny and sterile. I remember my shoes squeaking on the tiles.

The first thing I noticed when we entered the building was the smell of disinfectant, and as we climbed the stairs, the smell became overwhelming, seeping into the back of my throat and clogging my nostrils.

I stopped for a moment, finding it hard to breathe. I was not sure if it was the stench or the hard lump in the back of my throat. I was desperate to see Mammy, but terrified of what I would see at the same time.

Whilst I stood there, I felt as if I was invisible. Nurses marched past me, up and down the corridor, and out of numerous swing doors: their starched uniforms rustling as they walked; their metal trays, with their gleaming instruments rattling ominously. As one of the doors behind me swung open, the stench of disinfectant faded to be replaced by the smell of chicken stew. **It was tea-time, but for once I wasn't hungry.**

I watched as my father turned into a room at the end of the corridor. **For the first time, I saw him hesitate – his shoulders stooped.** Briefly, he looked back, gave me a quick nod, then turned and vanished into the room.

For a moment, I was rooted to the spot, taking quick shuddering breaths. In the distance, a trolley creaked, and cups rattled, **but they sounded muffled, distant, as if I was underwater. A door slamming somewhere behind me jolted me into action, and I started to move – almost robotically, focused on the open door.**

14

Dialogue

Dialogue is important to develop character, to make the character come to life on the page, but also to 'show' the reader what is happening in the story – to move the action along. It does, however, need to have a purpose and should only be included when it is necessary to add detail about the character and/or plot.

'Show not tell' is important in dialogue to help the reader visualise the scene. Body language is a crucial element as it gives the reader important clues that they can use to recreate the scene in their mind.

Tip: Keep the dialogue brief as long exchanges between characters slows the pace of the story.

Two components that add clarity and detail to dialogue are **dialogue tags** and **action beats**.

DIALOGUE TAGS

Dialogue tags attach the dialogue to a particular character. For example, 'I said,' or 'he growled.'

Examples

> "Rusty did bite me. Look!" I screamed.
> "He couldn't have hurt you," Mammy spluttered.

DOI: 10.4324/9781003215653-15

Using dialogue tags

a. Use a tag whenever it is unclear who is speaking. They are necessary to avoid confusion about who is speaking.

b. The dialogue itself is what is important. The tag is just functional and in lots of cases 'said' is fine, and there is no need to come up with alternative synonyms. However, they may be appropriate to indicate a tone of voice, for example, whispered, shouted, roared, snarled.

Example

"Was it you?" I could only nod. "Speak up girl," Mr Rogers roared.

c. Sometimes an adverb might suit the meaning better than changing the verb, for example, 'she said menacingly,' rather than 'she muttered,' but don't overdo it.

Example

"It won't last long," he said gently.

Position of dialogue tags

They can go before, during or after the dialogue. Changing their position creates a more varied flow and rhythm to the writing.

a. After the dialogue
   ☆ End dialogue with a comma, question mark, exclamation mark.
   ☆ The first letter of the tag is not a capital unless it is a name.

Examples

"Let me have a look," my mother said.
"Why is that so funny?" my sister asked.
"He did bite me. Look!" I screamed.
"Was it you?" Mr Rogers roared.

b. Before the dialogue
  ☆ Use a comma after the tag.
  ☆ Start the dialogue with a capital letter.

Examples

I screamed, "He did bite me. Look!"
Mr Rogers roared, "Was it you?"

c. During the dialogue
    If the dialogue is interrupted during a sentence:
  ☆ Use a comma after the tag.
  ☆ Start the next piece of dialogue with a lowercase letter.

Example

"Rusty might have tried to bite you," she said, "but he couldn't have hurt you."

ACTION BEATS

An action beat can be an action, thought or description. They are important to help the reader visualise the scene.

Examples

My sister looked at my hand. "Not a mark! Well, he couldn't have, because he would have left a mark," she said, dropping my hand in disgust, and stomping out of the room.

"I'm not going to school tomorrow," I said, still refusing to look at him. "Everyone will make fun of me."

I saw him glance at the upside-down tap in front of me, and he roared, "Was it you?" I could only nod. "Speak up, girl."

"Ye … Yes, ssir," I stammered. My mouth had gone dry, my tongue felt like a heavy lump of rubber and my bottom lip had started to tremble.

REVISION

When revising your first draft, check:

1. Is it clear who is speaking?
2. Are all the dialogue tags necessary?
3. Have you included action beats to add variety, detail and meaning to the scene?

EXERCISE

1. Create a comic strip of the scene.
2. Write the dialogue using speech bubbles.
3. Take the dialogue from the speech bubbles and insert it into the original paragraph.

15

Reflections

Reflections are the writer's thoughts about what they learned, gained, understood as a result of the event or experience. How it changed them.

EXERCISE

★ Write two or three sentences to sum up why your memory was important to you.

★ **For example:** I felt like a fool, but I realised that sometimes it is good to be able to laugh at yourself. I learned that even if you are the subject of gossip or ridicule, it won't last long.

Apprentice writers often find reflections hard to write. Providing the following starter can help give a structure until they become more experienced with the language of a reflection/memoir.

REFLECTION STARTER

In all our lives, there is a moment of reflection, a turning point. The incident with … made me realise that …

DOI: 10.4324/9781003215653-16

Examples

1. In all our lives there is a moment of reflection, a turning point. For me, the embarrassing incident with Rusty the Dog made me realise that sometimes it is good to be able to laugh at yourself. It also taught me that even if you are the subject of gossip or ridicule, it won't last forever. As my father said, "Today's news is tomorrow's fish and chip papers."

2. In all our lives there is a moment of regret, a moment of reflection, a turning point. For me, Mr Rogers' science laboratory was that place and the incident with the tap was when I learned to be a captain not a clown; learned that sometimes it is good to be invisible; learned that school is a place to learn not a stage for entertaining, but not through fear of Mr Rogers or any punishment, but the disappointment at having let down my parents and the headmaster.

   The story was retold hundreds of times that day. Everyone laughed raucously, except me who had a letter burning a hole in my satchel, waiting to be handed to my mam and dad. Their disappointment was far harder to bear than a rap on the knuckles. So was the fact that Mr Rogers now knew my name, and every lesson his eyes would be watching my every movement, like a predator watching its prey, waiting for me to make a wrong move, give a wrong answer. I was no longer invisible. I had his sole, undivided attention!

3. It was only the back of an exercise book from the last school year, but it was somewhere I could write, I could think, I could remember: somewhere I could remove the mask, somewhere I could be me.

   When I put down my pen, I was surprised to see that the ink was smudged, the paper damp, and my cheeks soaking wet. This was the first time I had cried since that awful day. I realised that the teacher was right. Writing is a powerful tool to examine your memories and express your feelings.

16

Editing

Whilst writing the first draft, don't pay any particular attention to punctuation as this will slow you down, and the main aim is to get the scene down on paper. Once you have written the first draft and revised it that is the time to examine the punctuation, sentence lengths and structures to produce a final draft.

TIPS

1. Reading the draft aloud, either to yourself or to an editing partner, is a useful way of picking up any errors.
2. When writing your first draft you should have:
   a. **Double spaced** your writing (only write on every other line) to leave enough room to edit your work.
   b. Left a **double margin** on the left-hand side. This can be used to make editing reminders.
   c. **Numbered your paragraphs**, so that you can tackle one paragraph at a time when editing the first draft.

The following editing model demonstrates the editing process. In the model, the editing actions are shown in the left-hand column to highlight the process. However, in your own writing marking the changes in the text and inserting a star in the left-hand margin will be sufficient to ensure that all edits are completed.

DOI: 10.4324/9781003215653-17

EDITING MODEL

Editing notes	Main text (Paragraph 1)
[1] Delete *from school* [2] No comma after *dog* [3] Substitute *and* for the comma	Walking home [1]**from school**, swinging my satchel, eyes fixed on the pavement, I was deep in thought about a difficult day at school. A sudden barking made me glance up. Mrs Thomas' **dog[2], was** at the gate, balanced on his hind legs, with his front legs gripping the top of the iron **gate,[3] wagging** his tail furiously.
Edited paragraph	Walking home, swinging my satchel, eyes fixed on the pavement, I was deep in thought about a difficult day at school. A sudden barking made me glance up. Mrs Thomas' **dog was** at the gate, balanced on his hind legs, with his front legs gripping the top of the iron **gate and** wagging his tail furiously.

Editing notes	Main text (Paragraph 2)
[1] Combine two sentences using *which* [2] Delete *seemed to* [3] *hung* not *hand* [4] *times* not *time*	The most peculiar thing about Rusty was his **mouth.[1] It was** surrounded by wiry, grey hairs and was permanently puckered as if he disapproved of everything and everyone. A silvery string of slimy drool **seemed to[2]** constantly **hand[3]** from the left-hand corner of his mouth. Sometimes, Rusty looked really pleased to see you, like today. Other **time[4]**, he would launch himself at the gate, yapping furiously, the hairs on his back stiff like a wire brush.

Edited paragraph	The most peculiar thing about Rusty was his **mouth, which was** surrounded by wiry, grey hairs and was permanently puckered as if he disapproved of everything and everyone. A silvery string of slimy drool constantly **hung** from the left-hand corner of his mouth. Sometimes, Rusty looked really pleased to see you, like today. Other **times,** he would launch himself at the gate, yapping furiously, the hairs on his back stiff like a wire brush.

Editing notes	Main text (Paragraph 5)
[1] Full stop after *look*. [2] New sentence *My mother…*	"Let me have **a look,**[1]" [2]**my** mother reached out to take my hand.
Edited text	"Let me have a look." My mother reached out to take my hand.

Editing notes	Main text (Paragraph 6)
[1] Substitute a comma for *and* [2] Change *clutched* to *clutching*	"No, don't touch me! It really hurts!" I shrieked **and**[1] **clutched**[2] my hand tighter to my chest.
Edited text	"No, don't touch me! It really hurts!" I shrieked, clutching my hand tighter to my chest.

EDITING PUNCTUATION

Full stops

When editing, read the text aloud and note when you pause with a mark at that point in your text. Ask:

★ Why did I pause?
★ Was it because:

A. The thought, statement, idea or description was complete?

B. I had to re-read what was written because it didn't make sense?

C. I have not marked the end of the sentence?

Capital letters

Check that you have used a capital letter:

* At the start of every sentence
* For names of people, places and I
* For days of the week and months of the year
* For titles of books, films, songs etc.

Question marks

Check that you have used a question mark:

* At the end of direct questions (where the exact words of the speaker are reported)

Exclamation marks

Check:

* Have you used too many exclamation marks? They should be for emphasis and to indicate a surprise, outburst or humour, and used sparingly.

Inverted commas

Check that you have:

* Used inverted commas to enclose the words a person says
* Used commas to separate the dialogue from the rest of the sentence
* Begun the dialogue with a capital letter
* Used question marks and exclamation marks inside the closing speech marks when appropriate
* Started a new line for each new speaker

Apostrophes: possession

Check you have:

*   ★ Used apostrophes to show possession (something belongs to someone)
*   ★ Have just added an apostrophe after the *s* for plural nouns
*   ★ Have just added an apostrophe after the *s* in singular nouns already ending in *s*

Apostrophes: contraction/omission

Check you have:

*   ★ Used apostrophes to show when two words have been joined together and some letters are missing
*   ★ Not confused it's/its, they're/their, you're/your
    *   ☆ It's = it is
    *   ☆ Its = belongs to it
    *   ☆ They're = they are
    *   ☆ Their = belonging to them
    *   ☆ You're = you are
    *   ☆ Your = belonging to you

Commas

Check you have used commas to separate:

*   ★ Items in a list
*   ★ Parts of a sentence to help make the meaning clear
*   ★ Extra information that is not essential to the meaning of the main part of the sentence

Comma splicing

Check that you have:

*   ★ Not used commas to join two complete sentences
*   ★ Used a conjunction to join two sentences

Appendix

Writing survey template
Writing survey model
The writing process from published writers
Modelled sentences: detail, flow, impact (DFI)
Rusty the Dog: a memoir
The Terrier Times
Mr Rogers: Science: Tales of Torture
Science: Tales of Torture: Messages
First Morning in Corfu
Sunrise on Corfu
Rwy'n Gartref [I am home]: description
Stunning Staycation: The Gower Peninsula
I'll Call Mammy
Floodland: Found Poem by Alison Wilcox, drawing from the novel
      by Marcus Sedgwick
The Sock Thief: A Moment of Frustration
Negativity in the Media: An Angry Response
Spider's web planning template
Scene/image box plan template
Scene/image box plan model
Fiction planning template
Fiction planning model
Character prompt card
Alison's Book Club
Research, articles, books and websites

Writing survey template

Experience of writing	
Who do you see writing?	
What and why are they writing?	
Who are they writing for?	
List all the kinds of writing you do.	
Why do you write?	
Who do you write for?	
Where do you write? Do you have a special notebook?	
Do you share your writing with anyone? Is there some writing that you like to keep private?	
Do you read other pupils' writings?	
What do you like about writing?	

What is your favourite kind of writing? What piece of writing are you most proud of?	
What do you not like about writing?	

The writing process

Do you find a blank page daunting? Do you struggle to start a piece of writing? How do you tackle this challenge?	
How do you plan your writing? Do you: a. Just like to get your ideas down on paper and want to start your first draft without too much planning? b. Like to use pictures and images, storyboards or webs? c. Prefer to plan in a methodical, detailed way, using an outline of each element of the story (setting, character, plot, problem and resolution) or topic?	
What helps you while you are writing? What makes it more difficult?	

What resources do you find helpful?	
Do you like to discuss how you could improve your writing with a teacher and/or a peer? What sort of feedback do you find helpful?	
Do you like to illustrate your writing or present it in different ways?	

Getting your ideas down onto paper	
What do you write with? Do you prefer to handwrite or type? Why?	
How would you describe the speed and legibility of your writing? (Can you get your ideas down on paper quickly and in a way that is **readable?**)	
Does the speed and look of your writing vary?	
Do you type fluently or are you a 'keyboard pecker'?	

Self-assessment	
What makes a piece of writing good?	
What makes a piece of writing poor?	
How do you rate yourself as a writer?	Poor Average Good Excellent
If you rated yourself as a poor writer, do you:	a. Say: "I'm rubbish at writing," do as little as possible, and avoid writing whenever you can. b. Say: "I want to get better," and find out what you need to do to improve. c. Work hard on the parts you find difficult, for example spelling, so that you improve.
If you rated yourself as an excellent writer, do you:	a. Write what you know you are good at. b. Tackle more challenging writing. c. Experiment with different styles, forms and techniques.
How would you rate your enjoyment of writing: don't like it, like it, love it?	Don't like it Like it Love it
What would you like to improve about your writing?	

What would help you to improve?	
What are your interests, hobbies, passions?	
Any other comments:	

Writing survey model

Experience of writing	
Who do you see writing?	Classmates, teachers, family
What and why are they writing?	School work, letters, lists, emails
Who are they writing for?	School, friends, family, business
List all the kinds of writing you do.	Letters, cards, essays, descriptive writing, test/exams, lists
Why do you write?	Because I have to!
Who do you write for?	Teachers, family, myself
Where do you write? Do you have a special notebook?	School books
Do you share your writing with anyone? Is there some writing that you like to keep private?	No
Do you read other pupils' writing?	Only at school
What do you like about writing?	Freedom of topics, writing what I like

What is your favourite kind of writing? What piece of writing are you most proud of?	Stories, narratives, personal experiences A challenge writing at school
What do you not like about writing?	Hand gets tired. I get stressed about what to write next. I struggle with grammar etc.

The writing process

Do you find a blank page daunting? Do you struggle to start a piece of writing? How do you tackle this challenge?	Yes I use sentence starters that my teacher gives me
How do you plan your writing? Do you: a. Just like to get your ideas down on paper and want to start your first draft without too much planning? b. Like to use pictures and images, storyboards or webs? c. Prefer to plan in a methodical, detailed way, using an outline of each element of the story (setting, character, plot, problem and resolution) or topic?	Get ideas down on paper
What helps you while you are writing? What makes it more difficult?	Typing helps, calm music Total silence doesn't normally help

What resources do you find helpful?	Pictures
Do you like to discuss how you could improve your writing with a teacher and/or a peer? What sort of feedback do you find helpful?	Yes, I talk to the teacher and it helps me How to plan and layout and spoken feedback
Do you like to illustrate your writing or present it in different ways?	No, I'd rather get it over and done with

Getting your ideas down onto paper

What do you write with? Do you prefer to handwrite or type? Why?	Fountain pen or biro I prefer to type. My hand doesn't hurt after typing
How would you describe the speed and legibility of your writing? (Can you get your ideas down on paper quickly and in a way that is **readable**?)	I write at a steady pace, if I rush it's not legible
Does the speed and look of your writing vary?	Yes all the time, different times in the day
Do you type fluently or are you a 'keyboard pecker'?	I'm getting better at typing

Self-assessment	
What makes a piece of writing good?	Readable, clear font, quality over quantity, interesting, subjects that interest me 'Everything I don't do'
What makes a piece of writing poor?	Messy writing, no punctuation, if it doesn't make sense 'Everything I do'
How do you rate yourself as a writer? If you rated yourself as a poor writer, do you:	Poor Used to be a, but now it's b. a. Say: "I'm rubbish at writing," do as little as possible, and avoid writing whenever you can. b. Say: "I want to get better," and find out what you need to do to improve. c. Work hard on the parts you find difficult, for example spelling, so that you improve.
If you rated yourself as an excellent writer, do you:	a. Write what you know you are good at. b. Tackle more challenging writing. c. Experiment with different styles, forms and techniques.

How would you rate your enjoyment of writing: don't like it, like it, love it?	Half and half Don't like it Like it
What would you like to improve about your writing?	Neatness, punctuation, getting ideas on paper
What would help you to improve?	Practising but I struggle with being bothered
What are your interests, hobbies, passions?	Rugby, skiing, camping, outdoor activities
Any other comments:	

The writing process from published writers

Floella Benjamin

An insightful and moving interview with Floella Benjamin about writing her memoir, *Coming to England*.

https://www.booktrust.org.uk/news-and-features/features/2016/october/floella-benjamin-on-coming-to-england-and-its-impact-20-years-on/

Michael Rosen

An interview with Michael Rosen about the research and writing of his 2019 book, *The Missing*. An essential read to understand the power of personal writing.

https://www.theguardian.com/lifeandstyle/2019/dec/28/michael-rosen-family-history-jewish-culture

Elizabeth Laird

This website is a treasure trove of ideas and resources. The 'Hello Teachers' section has background information about **Oranges in No Man's Land**, amongst others, which is a fascinating insight into the writing of the book.

http://www.elizabethlaird.co.uk/hello-teachers

J.K. Rowling – on planning

> It's like learning an instrument, you've got to be prepared for hitting wrong notes occasionally, or quite a lot, because I wrote an awful lot before I wrote anything I was really happy with … I have a large and complicated chart propped on the desk in front of me to remind me what happens where, how, to whom and which bits of crucial information need to be slipped into which innocent-looking chapters … I plan; I really plan quite meticulously.

https://thefriendlyeditor.com/2015/03/26/how-rowling-revised-harry-potter-phoenix/

Ray Bradbury

> The faster you blurt it out, the more swiftly you write, the more honest you are … In delay comes the effort for a style, instead of leaping upon truth which is the only style worth dead-falling and tiger-trapping.

David Walliams
Some top tips for apprentice writers.
https://www.explorelearning.co.uk/blog/david-walliams-top-ten-writing-tips/

Marcus Sedgwick
A photographic blog tour of the inspirations for his book *The Ghosts of Heaven* and his research.
https://www.theguardian.com/childrens-books-site/2014/oct/07/marcus-sedgwick-where-i-write-the-ghosts-of-heaven

Judith Kerr, interview on BBC Radio 4's 'Bookclub'
In this interview, Judith Kerr talks about why she decided to write *When Hitler Stole Pink Rabbit*. She discusses how she added details from her imagination to fill in the gaps in her memory and to make the story more dramatic.
www.bbc.co.uk/sounds/play/b050z2vc

Anthony Horowitz
This is an excellent resource for how to write a spy story, but the tips and resources are relevant to any genre, including personal writing.
https://www.bbc.co.uk/cbbc/joinin/bp-anthony-horowitz-spy-story-writing-masterclass

Shannon Hale

> I'm writing a first draft and reminding myself that I'm simply shovelling sand into a box, so that later, I can build castles.

Terry Pratchett

The first draft is just you telling yourself the story.

Judy Blume

The first draft is a skeleton … just bare bones. The rest of the story comes later with revising.

Modelled sentences

Detail, flow, impact (DFI)

These model sentences are provided as examples of target structures as outlined in the various Key Stage curricula, but more importantly, as examples and scaffolds to be discussed and explored, imitated and innovated to:

* rearrange ideas
* tinker with phrasing
* experiment with word choices
* try different sentence openers
* experiment with connectors
* make individual choices about preferred sentences in terms of clarity, rhythm and emphasis in the context of a paragraph

Technical knowledge of grammar without application will not improve a student's ability to construct precise, clear and powerful sentences that create an impact and are effective in the context of their text. Grammar and punctuation are part of a writer's 'toolkit'; knowledge of a variety of syntactic options when constructing sentences improves a writer's ability to apply those tools when crafting his or her own sentences to create different rhythms and emphasis, and for clarity, precision and power.

Exploring sentence options where there are a multitude of right answers is enjoyable as well as educational and will improve the students' ability to revise their own writing with an increasing variety of tools at their disposal. It is, in essence, coaching writing that values conversation and collaboration over correction, and exploration over explanation.

For those with more limited reading experience, working in collaboration with peers and a teacher can open their eyes to the repertoire of options available to express their ideas with clarity, detail and style. With practice in exploring effective sentences and the variety of linguistic options available, students are better equipped to revise their own texts. Writing out sentence choices that feel and sound right – ones that seem to work best in context – and recording these in their notebooks will provide models for future reference.

Example activities:

1. Students take a simple (kernel) sentence and develop detail by asking questions about what they would like to know. (See Chapter 13 for examples.)
2. Take a model sentence and experiment with different ways of structuring it. Then experiment with sentence openers, phrasing and word choice. Reading these sentences aloud enables students to hear the rhythm, and they can then collaborate to decide which option they prefer.

For example: "After the water from the tap crashed down from the ceiling, it soaked the bench in front."

Water crashed down from the ceiling. It soaked the bench in front.

Water crashed down from the ceiling, and it soaked the bench in front.

Water crashed down from the ceiling; it soaked the bench in front.

The water, which crashed down from the ceiling, soaked the bench in front.

Water crashed down from the ceiling – the front bench was soaked.

Down from the ceiling a deluge of water plunged and plummeted onto the heads of the bench in front.

Crashing down from the ceiling, the water soaked the bench in front.

The water crashed dramatically down from the ceiling to soak the bench in front.

The bench in front was soaked by the water crashing down from the ceiling.

The bench in front was soaked by the water crashing like a fountain down from the ceiling.

Like a fountain, a deluge of icy water cascaded down from the ceiling and soaked the bench in front.

Note: It is useful at this stage to remind students that the goal is good, clear, effective sentences that fit into the rhythm of the text and not complex, overcrowded sentences. Sometimes, brevity is the better option. The key is to experiment and develop a knowledge and understanding of the options that are available.

Simple sentences: statements, questions, commands

I was nervous of Mrs Thomas' dog.
He was a terrier.
Drool hung from the corner of his mouth.
I edged closer to the gate.
A low growl came from the back of his throat.
I grabbed my satchel.
Rusty lunged.
I clutched my hand to my chest.
My mother collapsed into fits of laughter.
Events had taken a strange turn.
I thrust my hand towards my mother.
Rusty couldn't have hurt you.
He doesn't have any teeth.
How could I face the neighbours?
How would I endure the weeks of teasing?
What happened?
Why is that so funny?
He did attack me! He did!
It really hurts!
Don't touch it.
Show me your hand.
March into school tomorrow.
Hold your head held high.
Laugh with them.

Noun phrases, expanded noun phrases (ENPs) and similes

The **small, stocky terrier** was yappy and temperamental.

He was **a small, stocky terrier with a red and brown curly coat, small dark beady eyes and** *pointy ears like a fox.*

His mouth was surrounded by **wiry, grey bristly hairs**.

A **silvery, string of slimy drool** hung from the corner of his mouth.

The hairs on the back of his neck were *stiff like a wire brush*.

A **low, warning growl** came from the back of his throat.

With a **high-pitched howl**, I grabbed my satchel.

Even my sister couldn't miss my **blotchy face** and **red-rimmed eyes**.

I often returned home from school with **torn tights, bleeding hands and knees**.

Hurt pride can be more painful than an **injured hand**.

He had a mouth *as sour as a rhubarb tart*.

His knuckles *cracked like a pistol shot*.

Relative clauses

I kept my hand as steady as possible, **which was not easy as my heart was racing**.

My mother, **who had been standing in the front window**, quickly hurried to the back door to meet me.

I sat waiting for my mother to return, **which she did within a few minutes**.

My sister, **who had taken my hand to examine it**, dropped it abruptly, and stomped out of the room in disgust.

I doubted I would ever leave the house and face the neighbours, **who must have heard me screeching all the way home**.

The children in the street, **who all went to the same school**, were bound to spread the story.

The physics teacher, **who was called Mr Rogers**, was a tyrant.

The teacher **who occupied the science laboratory** was a terror and a bully.

The most loathsome thing about Mr Rogers was the sweat, **which stained his shirt in numerous places**.

The sweat, **which erupted from every pore**, beaded his upper lip and his forehead.

The sweat, **which trickled down his forehead**, settled in his bushy eyebrows.

I tried to stifle the laughter **that was threatening to erupt in my throat**.

I hid in the bedroom **where I could escape the humiliation**.

Mr Rogers, **whose shadow I had spotted spreading over the bench**, was waiting for me to look up.

The laboratory had one terrible drawback, **which transformed it from a centre of discovery to a chamber of horrors**.

He marched over to his enormous desk, **which was covered in trays spilling wire and tubes**.

Fronted adverbials

Outside the laboratory, the sun was shining on the playing fields.

Inside the classroom, there was an atmosphere of gloom.

Behind Mr Rogers, the blackboard was covered in his spidery writing and complicated diagrams.

In the middle of the bench, the swivelling tap beckoned to me.

Suddenly, a spectacular fountain of water spurted out of the tap.

Hurriedly, we took our seats.

Eventually, he snarled, "Get out! I'll deal with you later."

For one brief moment, I thought I had got away with it.

Within a few minutes, my mother had returned.

Carefully, I slid my fingers towards the tap.

As innocently as I could, I stared at my exercise book.

Frantically, everyone grabbed their books and pencil cases.

Sometimes, Rusty looked really pleased to see you.

Other times, he would launch himself menacingly at the gate.

Slowly, I reached out my hand.

Finally, my mother managed to get herself under control.

Prepositional phrases

My eyes were fixed **on the pavement**.

Mrs Thomas' dog was **at the gate**.

A slimy string of drool hung **from the left-hand corner of his mouth**.

I edged closer **to the gate**.

I leaned **over the gate**.

I reached **out my right hand**.

From the back of his throat came a low growl.

I clutched my hand **to my chest**.

Out of the house she charged and marched **down the road to Mrs Thomas' house**.

I waited **in the kitchen**.

She stood **in front of me**, hands **on her hips**.

I thrust my hand **towards my mother**.

Tears streamed **down her cheeks**.

I heard my father's heavy tread **on the stairs**.

He poked his head **through the door**.

Underneath his arms were damp and stained.

The sweat erupted **from his pores** and beaded his upper lip.

Down his forehead the sweat trickled to settle **in his enormous, bushy eyebrows**.

We slunk **towards one of the long wooden benches**.

Behind Mr Rogers was his favourite piece of equipment – the blackboard.

I slid my fingers **towards the tap**.

A spectacular fountain of water exploded **out of the tap**, crashed **into the ceiling** and curved **downwards** to drop its heavy load **onto the head of Katie Evans**.

Everyone **on the front bench** leapt to their feet.

We watched as the water poured **from the bench** to collect **in puddles on the laboratory floor**.

Erupting **across his face**, the red patches were a sure signal that he was about to explode.

Coordinating conjunctions

His name was Rusty, **and he was yappy and temperamental.**

His front legs were gripping the top of the iron gate, **and he was wagging his tail madly.**

I swung my satchel off my shoulder **and edged closer to the gate.**

I stopped for a moment **and checked that his tail was still wagging.**

A low growl came from the back of his throat, **and I jerked my hand back.**

My mother had been in the window watching for my return from school, **but she would have heard my shrieks from the back of the house.**

My sister was showing me sympathy, **but my mother was laughing hysterically.**

Rusty might have gone for Alison, **but he couldn't possibly have bitten her.**

My hand might not have been hurt, **but my pride certainly was.**

I knew my father was standing in the doorway, **but I kept my eyes fixed to the floor.**

Outside, the sun was shining on the playing fields, **but inside, there was an atmosphere of gloom.**

"Are you listening, **or are you just plain stupid, girl**?"

I hadn't been sure that the tap would still swivel, **or if it would work upside down.**

It was an exciting discovery, **so we talked animatedly about it all day.**

Kathryn realised that I was ignoring her warning look, **so she slid her seat further away from mine.**

My sister was disgusted, **so she dropped my hand and stomped out of the room.**

We were eager to find out if the tap would work upside down, **so we agreed that we would try it next lesson.**

I knew he was leaning menacingly over the desk, **yet I could feel laughter bubbling at the back of my throat.**

It was an incredibly boring lesson of copying tortuous diagrams, **so I decided to find out what would happen if I swivelled the tap** *and turned it on*.

The front bench leapt out of their seats, **and they all made a grab for their books and pencil cases** *so they wouldn't be soaked as well*.

I kept my head down **and my eyes covered by my fringe**, *so that he couldn't see the excitement in my eyes*.

Subordinate clauses

Alison came home screaming **because Rusty had bitten her**.

He couldn't have bitten you **because he would have left a mark**.

Sometimes, people make fun **because they want to embarrass you**.

He never welcomed us **when we entered the class**.

When I looked closer, I noticed that my mother's shoulders were shaking.

When she asked what had happened, my mother collapsed into fits of laughter.

When he straightened his fingers to prepare for a blow, you couldn't help but notice his knuckles.

When we turned it on, we discovered that the tap could turn 360°.

Before the incident with the tap, I was just one of a sea of faces.

After the incident with the swivelling tap, I was well and truly on his radar.

After the water from the tap crashed down from the ceiling, it soaked the bench in front.

During a science experiment, my group realised that the tap in our sink was loose.

While the rest of the class were busy grabbing their possessions, I sat motionless on my seat.

All manner of painful tortures raced through my head **while I waited for him to act**.

While we were occupied in clearing up the mess, we didn't have time to worry about the consequences.

If I had been invisible before, I knew I now had Mr Rogers' undivided attention.

If I'd wanted to liven up the physics lesson, I had certainly succeeded.

If I was in any doubt, the demonic look in Mr Rogers' eyes was a stark warning of what was to come.

As a low growl came from the back of his throat, I jerked my hand back.

I jerked my hand back **as a low growl came from the back of his throat**.

As I shrieked, I clutched my hand tightly to my chest.

I could imagine the scene **as my mother berated Mrs Thomas about the incident**.

As she stood in front of me, I noticed that her mouth twitched slightly.

My mother hopped up and down **as she tried to put her shoes on at a run**.

As my mother collapsed into fits of laughter, I assumed she was suffering from some sort of meltdown.

I assumed she was suffering from some sort of meltdown **as my mother collapsed into fits of laughter**.

As I thrust my hand towards my mother, I noticed there wasn't a mark on it.

I noticed there was no bite mark on my hand **as I thrust my hand towards my mother**.

I vowed that I would stay in my room **until everyone had forgotten about the humiliating incident**.

Until everyone had forgotten the humiliating incident, I vowed not to leave my room.

I had a letter burning a hole in my satchel **until the time came to hand it over to my parents**.

Although I was in deep trouble for my stupidity, I had learned a valuable lesson that day.

Participle phrases

Walking home, swinging my satchel, eyes fixed on the pavement, I was in deep thought about a difficult day at school.

He would launch himself at the gate, **yapping furiously**, with hairs bristling on the back of his neck like a wire brush.

Swinging my satchel off my shoulder, I edged closer to the gate.

I leaned over the gate, **keeping my eyes fixed on Rusty, watching for any sign that he was feeling bad-tempered**.

I reached out a little further, **keeping my hand as steady as possible**.

Keeping my hand as steady as possible, I reached out a little further.

Grabbing my satchel, nursing my hand to my chest, I sobbed all the way home.

I looked intently at my exercise book, **praying that he didn't notice that I wasn't holding my pencil**.

A spectacular fountain exploded out of the tap, **crashing into the ceiling and curving downwards to drop its heavy load on to the head of Katie Evans**.

Parentheses

The physics teacher, **a tall, pot-bellied, red-faced old tyrant**, was a terror and a bully.

The most loathsome thing about Mr Rogers was the sweat that erupted from every pore – **underneath his arms, his stomach and chest** – staining his crumpled shirt.

His hands **(enormous and shovel-like)** were lethal.

We always stopped for a brief glance at the glass cabinets full of exciting equipment, **test tubes and glass jars full of brightly coloured chemicals**, before slinking to one of the long wooden benches.

Kathryn stared at me in horror and shook her head **(she knew I could never resist a dare)** and edged her chair further away from mine.

Semicolons

A low growl came from the back of his throat; **I jerked my hand back**.

Strangely, my sister was showing me sympathy; **my mother was laughing hysterically**.

My sister was disgusted; **she dropped my hand and stomped out of the room**.

I knew my father was standing in the doorway; **I kept my eyes fixed to the floor**.

Outside, the sun was shining on the playing fields; **inside, there was an atmosphere of gloom**.

It was an exciting discovery; **we talked animatedly about it all day**.

Kathryn realised that I was ignoring her warning look; **she slid her seat further away from mine**.

Colons

The most peculiar thing about Rusty was his mouth: **permanently puckered with a silvery string of slimy drool hanging from the left-hand corner of his mouth**.

I jerked my hand back: **not quick enough**.

She stood in front of me: **hands on hips, one eyebrow slightly raised.**

There was a mark on my hand: **a blob of silvery drool, but no bite mark**.

My sister looked at my hand: **not a mark**.

It was his hands that disturbed us most: **enormous, shovel-like, with nails like jagged claws**.

IMPACT

Changing the order

My mother hopped up and down as she tried to put her shoes on at a run.

As she tried to put her shoes on at a run, my mother hopped up and down.

Rusty would launch himself at the gate, yapping furiously.

Yapping furiously, Rusty would launch himself at the gate.

I reached out a little further, keeping my hand as steady as possible.

Keeping my hand as steady as possible, I reached out a little further.

Nursing my hand, I sobbed all the way home.

I sobbed all the way home, nursing my hand.

Before the incident with the swivelling tap, I was just one of a sea of faces.

I was just one of a sea of faces before the incident with the swivelling tap.

He never welcomed us when we entered the classroom.

When we entered the classroom, he never welcomed us.

Opening adjectives and similes

Small and stocky, the terrier was yappy and temperamental.
Enormous and shovel-like, his hands were menacing, as were his jagged nails.
Tall, pot-bellied and red-faced, Mr Rogers was a bully and a terror.
Stale and garlicky, the stench of his sweat was nauseous.

Delayed adjectives

The terrier, **small and stocky**, was yappy and temperamental.
His hands, **enormous and shovel-like**, were menacing, as were his jagged nails.
Mr Rogers, **tall, pot-bellied and red-faced**, was a bully and a terror.
The stench of his sweat, **stale and garlicky**, was nauseous.

Opening adverbs

Carefully, I slid my fingers towards the tap.
Frantically, everyone grabbed their books and pencil cases.
Slowly, I reached out my hand.
Finally, my mother managed to get herself under control.
Soon, I would have to face my parents' disappointment.
Suddenly, a spectacular fountain of water spurted out of the tap.
Somehow, I would have to find the courage to face the rest of the world.
Gradually, the consequences of what I had just done began to dawn on me.

Delayed adverbs

I slid my fingers **carefully** towards the tap.
Everyone **frantically** grabbed their books and pencil cases.
I reached out my hand **slowly**.
My mother **finally** managed to get herself under control.
I would **soon** have to face my parents' disappointment.

A spectacular fountain of water **suddenly** spurted out of the tap.

I would **somehow** have to find the courage to face the rest of the world.

The consequences of what I had just done began **gradually** to dawn on me.

Compound verbs

I **swung my satchel** off my shoulder and **edged closer** to the gate.

I **leaned over the gate, kept my eyes fixed on Rusty,** and **watched for any sign** that he was going to attack.

I **reached out my hand, stopped for a moment,** and **checked that his tail was still wagging.**

My mother **grabbed her shoes, hopped up and down** as she tried to put them on, **charged out of the house** and **marched down the road.**

We **stopped for a moment, lingered longingly at the glass cabinets** and then, **slunk to our benches.**

Keeping my eye on Mr Rogers, I **slid my fingers towards the tap,** and **twisted it** until the spout faced the ceiling.

He **whipped around, scanned the class,** and then **stared directly at me.**

Kathryn **stared at me in horror, shook her head, and edged her seat further away from mine.**

A fountain of water **spurted out of the tap, crashed into the ceiling,** and **cascaded downwards** onto the head of Katie Evans.

Rusty the Dog
A memoir

Walking home, swinging my satchel, eyes fixed on the pavement, I was deep in thought about a difficult day at school. A sudden barking made me glance up. Mrs Thomas' dog was at the gate, balanced on his hind legs, with his front legs gripping the top of the iron gate and wagging his tail madly.

I was nervous of Mrs Thomas' dog. His name was Rusty, and he was yappy and temperamental. He was a small, stocky terrier, with a red and brown curly coat, small dark beady eyes and pointy ears like a fox. The most peculiar thing about Rusty was his mouth, which was surrounded by wiry, grey hairs and was permanently puckered as if he disapproved of everything and everyone. A silvery string of slimy drool hung from the left-hand corner of his mouth. Sometimes, Rusty looked really pleased to see you, like today. Other times, he would launch himself at the gate, yapping furiously, the hairs on his back stiff like a wire brush.

Swinging my satchel off my shoulder, I edged closer to the gate. I leaned over the gate, keeping my eyes fixed on Rusty, watching for any sign that he was feeling bad-tempered. Slowly, I reached out my right hand, stopped for a moment, checked that his tail was still wagging. It was. I reached out a little further. Keeping my hand as steady as possible, which was not easy as my heart was racing, I moved my hand closer for him to sniff. A low growl came from the back of his throat; I jerked my hand back. Not quick enough. Snarling, Rusty lunged.

With a high-pitched howl, I grabbed my satchel, and nursing my hand to my chest, sobbed the fifty or so metres to my house. My mother had been in the window watching for my return from school, but even if she had been at the back of the house, she would have heard my shrieks and sobs.

"Rusty's bitten me!" I wailed.

"Let me have a look." My mother reached out to take my hand.

"No, don't touch it! It really hurts!" I shrieked, clutching my hand tighter to my chest.

My mother grabbed her shoes, hopped up and down as she tried to put them on at a run, then charged out of the house and marched down the road to Mrs

Thomas'. I could imagine the scene as my mother berated Mrs Thomas about her nasty, vicious dog who had bitten me.

I was too busy sobbing to examine my hand and sat waiting in the kitchen until my mother returned, which she did within a few minutes.

Something strange had happened in Mrs Thomas'. My mother had changed. She stood in front of me, hands on her hips, one eyebrow slightly raised. I was somewhat bemused. Definitely no sympathy. Then, I noticed that the corner of her mouth twitched ever so slightly. She didn't move, just stood there looking at me. I was so confused by her change in attitude that I stopped screeching.

When I looked closely at my mother, I noticed that her shoulders were shaking, and her lips were pursed tightly together as if to stifle a laugh. I was now deeply offended. Being bitten by a dog was no laughing matter. What on earth had happened to my mother in Mrs Thomas' house!

With that, my sister arrived home from school. She saw me nursing my hand and realised that I had been crying. Even my sister couldn't miss the blotchy face and red-rimmed eyes. I was well-known for getting into scrapes on the way back from school, and often returned home with torn tights, bleeding hands and knees. She merely assumed that I'd had yet another accident. When she asked what had happened, my mother collapsed into fits of laughter. My mother was clearly suffering from some sort of meltdown.

"Alison came home screaming because Rusty, Mrs Thomas' dog, had bitten her." Here, she had to stop because she could hardly talk in between the hysterical laughter.

"Why is that so funny?" my sister asked.

Events had taken a very strange turn. My sister was showing me more sympathy than my mother. I think she too thought my mother had gone insane.

"Because when I went to see Mrs Thomas, she told me that Rusty may have gone for Alison, but he couldn't possibly have bitten her." My mother collapsed into a chair, clutching her stomach.

"He did bite me. Look," I screamed, removing my hand from the safety of my chest, and thrusting it towards my mother. To my shock, there wasn't a mark on my hand, just a blob of silvery drool.

With that, my mother could not speak a word. Tears streamed down her cheeks and she gasped for breath between laughter that seemed to shake her whole body.

"But he did attack me!" I yelled, indignantly. "He did!"

My sister looked at my hand. Not a mark. "Well, he couldn't have because he would have left a mark," she said, dropping my hand in disgust, and stomping out of the room.

Eventually, my mother managed to get herself sufficiently under control to speak. "Rusty might have tried to bite you," she said, "but he couldn't have hurt you." Choking with laughter, she spluttered, "Because he has no teeth."

My hand might have not been hurt, but my pride most certainly was. I grabbed my satchel, stormed upstairs, slammed my door and slumped on my bed, wondering how on earth I was going to be able to face the neighbours. Every one of them must have heard me screeching all the way up the road. Hurt pride can be more painful than an injured hand. The fact that all the children in the street went to the same school ensured that the story would spread, and I would have to endure days of teasing. I didn't think I could ever face anyone again and refused to come out of my room even when I heard my father return from work.

I heard his heavy tread on the stairs, and knew he was coming to 'have a talk with me.' Slowly, my door inched open. I kept my eyes fixed to the carpet, unable to look at my father. He poked his head through the door and asked if I was okay.

"I'm not going to school tomorrow," I said, still refusing to look at him. "Everyone will make fun of me."

"It won't last long," he said, gently. "Remember what I told you about today's news being tomorrow's fish and chip papers? Sometimes, people make fun because they want to embarrass you, and are being nasty. Sometimes, it's because it is a funny story, and they can't help but laugh. I suggest that you march into school, tell your friends the story, and laugh with them. It will soon be forgotten."

I took my father's advice, and surprisingly, found myself genuinely laughing along with the rest of my schoolmates.

By Alison Wilcox (2019)

The Terrier Times

www.petstories.com   THE PET NEWSPAPER OF THE YEAR   12th June 1975

SHOCKING!

ELDERLY DOG LEFT TRAUMATISED AFTER INCIDENT WITH YOUTH
by Larry Labrador

Rusty, an aged terrier, was left traumatised yesterday after he was falsely accused of biting a twelve-year-old local youth.

Known to be nervous because of his poor eyesight, the terrier, Rusty, went to greet the youth on her way home from school.

A sudden movement by the youth, identified as Miss Alison Wilcox, terrified Rusty, who lunged at the girl. The pandemonium that ensued after the unfortunate incident resulted in Rusty taking to his bed, quivering with fright. He has refused to leave the house ever since.

In an interview today, Mrs Thomas, Rusty's owner commented:

"Rusty is an old dog, partially blind and has no teeth. Rusty would never bite anyone, and even if he did, he has no teeth for goodness- sake. The only victim here is Rusty. To be falsely accused of biting Alison, whose high-pitched shrieks could be heard two streets away, has left Rusty distraught.

To prevent such incidents occurring in the future, which could affect the long-term mental health of our pets, it is vital that young people are taught how to approach pets responsibly and not to over-dramatize a situation.

Mrs Wilcox, Alison's mother, suggested that an apology might resolve the situation, but the damage has already been done."

Mrs Mahoney, a neighbour and a witness to the incident told us:

"I was standing in the window, watching the kids come home from school, when I heard an unearthly shrieking from the bottom of the street and saw Alison running up the road, clutching her hand. Shortly afterwards, I witnessed her mother charging down the road to Mrs Thomas' house.

Earlier I had seen Alison stop at Mrs Thomas' gate and lean over to pat Rusty. It was only a split second later when pandemonium broke out.

Speaking to some of the other neighbours, I discovered that Alison had accused Rusty of biting her. I was shocked. Everyone in this street knows that Rusty has no teeth.

I was saddened to hear that Rusty has been left terribly shaken by this incident."

Miss Wilcox, a pupil at the local comprehensive school, refused to comment on the incident.

A happy, confident Rusty pictured before the unfortunate incident.

A source close to Miss Wilcox commented that, "Alison is extremely embarrassed by the incident, but she had genuinely been under the impression that she had been bitten. She regrets that Rusty was in any way affected by the incident and hopes that he will soon regain his confidence."

Peter Pekinese from the Pet Protection League has called for this matter to be raised at the next sitting of the Alsatian Assembly. "It is time that the Assembly was seen to be taking steps to educate the youth of today about the impact of false accusations."

Mr Rogers: Science: Tales of Torture

The Incident of the Swivelling Tap

In all our lives there is a moment of regret, a moment of reflection, a turning point. For me, Mr Rogers' science laboratory was that place: the moment I learned to be a captain, not a clown; learned that sometimes it is good to be invisible; learned that school is a place to be educated, not a stage for entertaining.

The physics lab in the year 1977 was the very centre of our torture. To us it was what the Tower of London was to treasonous dukes and earls, or the ducking chair was to a witch. Without it, our lives would have been carefree. The lab was state-of-the-art, equipped with all sorts of interesting equipment, potions and powders. But it had one terrible drawback, which transformed it from a centre of discovery to a chamber of horrors. The teacher who occupied it was a terror and a bully. We hated him and we had good reason for doing so.

His name was Mr Rogers. He was a tall, pot-bellied, red-faced old bully with bristly hairs that stuck out of his ears and waggled from his nose when he shouted. He had a mouth as sour as a rhubarb tart, and he always scowled. Never once did he greet us or even acknowledge us when we entered the class, and the only times he spoke to us directly was to shout things like, "Are you listening, or are you thick, girl?" Or "Stop talking, girl, and you might be able to get some of the questions right for a change."

But the most loathsome thing about Mr Rogers was the sweat that clung to him. Underneath his arms were damp and stained. His shirt was creased and stuck to his stomach and chest in crinkled patches. It erupted from his pores like the fury he vented on us, beading his upper lip and his forehead, trickling down to settle in his bushy eyebrows that met in the middle and stuck out fiercely at odd angles.

It was his hands, however, that disturbed us most, his enormous shovel-like hands, with nails like jagged claws. They were lethal and were forever gripping some weapon, be it ruler or blackboard rubber. And do not forget please that it was those hands and fingers that were meant to be used to educate us in the wonders of science, not the pain from the thwack of a ruler. When he straightened his fingers to prepare for a blow, you couldn't help noticing the knuckles. They were misshapen as if he had been a bare-knuckle fighter in his youth and, cracked like a pistol shot before he cuffed one of us around the head. There were few precious laws to protect kids in those days, and nobody, least of all me, ever thought of telling our parents or another teacher of our daily torment.

You would be right in wondering why anyone would be stupid enough to provoke this monster? Well, I was, and did I suffer for that one moment of madness. Before the incident with the tap, to Mr Rogers we were just another sea of faces. He took out his frustration at our 'stupidity' indiscriminately. Nobody came in for special attention. But all that changed.

During a science experiment, my group realised that the tap in our sink was loose. When we turned it, we discovered that it could turn 360 degrees. It was an exciting discovery and we talked animatedly all day about whether the tap would still work if we turned it on. We agreed that one day we would try.

When we entered the science lab, we always lingered: stopped for a moment to glance at the glass cabinets full of test tubes and glass jars full of brightly coloured chemicals, and trays of wires and tubes, bulbs and batteries and many other fascinating equipment. Outside, the sun was shining on the playing fields, but inside there was an atmosphere of gloom. We slunk towards one of the long wooden benches and hurriedly took our seats as Mr Rogers stomped into the room. He marched over to his enormous wooden desk, which was covered in trays spilling wires and tubes and all sorts of paraphernalia: a tub of different coloured chalks; a huge wooden ruler; two board rubbers (one for use on the chalkboard, the other as a missile to attract the attention of anyone who wasn't paying attention), and stacks and stacks of exercise books awaiting his red pen. Behind him was his favourite piece of equipment: an enormous blackboard covered in his spidery writing and complicated diagrams.

We scrambled in our bags for books and pencil cases but stole quick, eager looks at the glass cases. Maybe today we would get a chance to experiment with the equipment. Any hope quickly faded as Mr Rogers ordered us to copy the diagram drawn on the board. It was a particularly boring lesson, copying those tortuous, complicated diagrams, so I decided to find out what would happen if I swivelled the tap and turned it on.

Mr Rogers was busy chalking another diagram on the board, the chalk screeching as he labelled the various parts. His back was turned. Keeping my eye on Mr Rogers, I slid my fingers towards the tap and twisted it until the spout faced the ceiling. He seemed to have an instinct for anyone not studiously working in his lesson and at the slightest noise he would whip round, his fierce blue eyes scanning the class. I held my breath and looked intently at my exercise book, praying that he didn't notice that I wasn't holding my pencil. His eyes narrowed for a moment, and then he turned his back and continued with his diagram.

Everyone on my bench was watching excitedly to see what I would do next. Most were grinning, anticipatory. Would the tap still work? What would happen if it did? I glanced at Beverley, who was grinning from ear to ear and mouthed to me, "Go on. Turn it on."

Kathryn stared at me in horror and shook her head, her eyes wide with panic (she knew I never could resist a dare). When she realised that I was ignoring her, Kathryn edged her seat further away from mine. She didn't want to have anything to do with this prank.

Never in my wildest dreams could I have imagined the carnage that followed. I wasn't even convinced that the tap could work upside down. I thought at best there would be a trickle of water, possibly onto the floor. Never did I foresee such a spectacular fountain of water spurting out of that tap, crashing into the ceiling and curving downwards to drop its heavy load on to the head of Katie Evans and the bench directly in front. The bench was soaked, exercise books, textbooks, pencil cases all sodden. Everyone on the front bench had leapt to their feet, screaming, grabbing their books and pencil cases, watching as the water poured from the bench to collect in puddles on the laboratory floor.

Mr Rogers spun round, his eyes narrowed to slits, his mouth a thin, terrifying line. Red patches spread across his face. For a moment, he didn't say a word, and then he started roaring instructions. For a while, we were all too occupied in clearing up the mess to worry about Mr Rogers, that is, all except me. My stomach was turning somersaults; my heart was thudding in my chest.

When we were all seated again, Mr Rogers stood legs apart, arms behind his back, glaring at each of us in turn. He had already worked out that the culprit was someone on the second bench. My friends stared at their books, too afraid to meet his fierce stare. Even though my legs were trembling, for some reason, I could feel a giggle bubbling in my throat. I couldn't take my eyes off the drenched figure of Katie Evans. Water trickled down her usually immaculate plaits and her blue ribbons drooped sorrowfully. I bit my lower lip to stifle the laughter that threatened to erupt.

Mr Rogers' gaze fixed on me. Slowly, he walked towards the bench, stood directly in front of me, gripped the desk with his enormous hands and leant over. The stench of stale sweat and garlic was overwhelming, and I desperately wanted to cover my nose and mouth. But I didn't dare move. I saw him glance at the upside-down tap in front of me, and he roared, "Was it you?" I could only nod. "Speak up, girl."

"Ye…Yes, ssir," I stammered. My bottom lip had started to tremble.

"What's your name?" he growled. For a moment, I couldn't speak. You could hear a pin drop. It was as if the whole class was holding their breath. The table shook as he slammed his hand on the desk.

"Wilcox, sir." I couldn't look up, but kept my eyes fixed to my book. I knew he hadn't picked up the ruler, but all manner of painful tortures raced through my head while I waited for him to act.

To my surprise, he merely snarled, "Get out! I'll deal with you later."

The story was retold hundreds of times that day. Everyone laughed raucously, except me. I had a letter burning a hole in my satchel, waiting to be handed to my mam and dad. Their disappointment was far harder to bear than a wrap on the knuckles. So was the fact that Mr Rogers now knew my name, and every lesson his eyes would be watching my every movement, like a predator watching its prey, waiting for me to make a wrong move, give a wrong answer. I was no longer invisible. I had his sole, undivided attention!

Science: Tales of Torture

Messages

MESSAGE BOARD: THE BAFFLED PHYSICISTS

THE LEGEND STRIKES AGAIN!

Greetings everyone. For those baffled physicists who missed today's physics lesson for a music exam, WOW, you missed an absolute corker.

You remember the swivelling tap we discovered last lesson. It works upside down!! No-one thought Alison would actually turn it on. But she did. LEGEND!

You should have seen the deluge that hit the ceiling and cascaded down onto the serious scientists. SPECTACLE!!!

Mind you, I wouldn't want to be in Alison's shoes next lesson, or any other future physics lesson come to that. Mr Rogers has well and truly MARKED HER CARD. The demented look in his eye was TERRIFYING!!!

MESSAGE BOARD: THE SERIOUS SCIENTISTS

GRAVE CONSEQUENCES AS GRAVITY STRIKES

Dear Serious Scientists,

For those of you who missed today's physics lesson, it was a nightmare. Wilcox was a buffoon as usual. Instead of focusing on the lesson, she turned on the swivelling tap. All of us in the front row were soaked. My textbook is a soggy mess and I have to wait for it to dry out to do my homework (unless anyone can lend me theirs).

Mr Rogers was apoplectic. I thought I would have to administer CPR. He sent Wilcox out of the class. Trust me, she is in serious bother and will have to toe the line now. At least those of us who want to learn won't have to suffer her juvenile disruptions any longer.

First Morning in Corfu

The cockerel choir has started up, crowing, "Get up. Open your windows. Come and see the dawn." They are loud, persistent, their echoes rebounding across the valley.

Slowly, sluggishly, one eye half-closed, I crawl out of bed and make my way to the balcony, murmuring under my breath about being woken up so early on the first day of my holiday.

Standing on the balcony, I am immediately entranced by the scene. The sun is just peeking over the horizon and painting thin, wispy strands of peach across the sky. Gradually, the bands thicken and spread as the sun rises. In the distance, the mysterious shadow of the Albanian hills is just visible, shrouded by a layer of mist. Then, as if dawn has exploded, it fills the sky with its blazing bright orange light.

As the sun continues to rise, the cockerels go quiet. The morning sea begins to stir. A crystalline shimmer spreads across its surface as if nature's fairy lights have suddenly been turned on. A gentle breeze springs up and rustles in the huge cypress trees below, then ripples across the surface of the sea, sending waves to swish and slosh onto the beach.

What a glorious welcome to Corfu. There is a glow, a warmth, an anticipation tingling in my veins. I'm ready to start the day.

By Alison Wilcox (2019)

Sunrise on Corfu

A HAIKU

Sun peeks over hills.
Morning sea stirs lazily.
Shimmering ripples.

A CINQUAIN

Sunrise
Peach strands
Rising, spreading, exploding
Shimmering glow, glorious warmth
Anticipation

By Alison Wilcox (2019)

Rwy'n Gartref [I am home]: description

It feels good to be back after all this time. For the first time in months, I feel free. The precarious scramble down the steep winding path has been worth the effort, and I have chosen a great day to revisit old memories. Not much has changed. Steep, craggy cliffs surround the cove on all sides. The only difference is the pile of huge boulders that nestle at the base of the south cliff, evidence of the tragic cliff collapse decades ago. The small, sheltered cove is deserted now, not like in the past.

Today, the sun blazes from a brilliant blue sky over a sea that shimmers as if crystals have been sprinkled between the ripples: its warmth wrapping round my body like a fleecy blanket.

I throw off my shoes, feel the sun-dappled sand between my toes. For a moment, I stand still and listen to the waves crashing against the cliffs.

Shells tossed by the tide, scattered treasures of years gone by, lead me to the water's edge. I close my eyes, inhale deeply and savour those memories. I rejoice at the salty smell of the ocean spray that is curling and lapping at my feet. The wind tugs my hair from its band, sending it dancing wildly. As I stand there, I can hear children laughing, splashing in the shallows and sending water over the shivering shilly-shalliers. They call to one another and I can see them plunging through the waves into the cold depths. That was a long time ago. Now when a wave surges onto the beach and breaks into circles of dancing water to soak the bottom of my trousers, it sends me scampering back onto dry land.

Today, except for the soothing swish, splash and slosh of the waves, there is no other sound. No birds singing. No voices of excited children playing on the beach.

As I walk back to the cliffs, I wriggle my toes so that the golden sand trickles over my feet. I feel like the only person on earth as I wrap those memories around me like an old, comforting blanket. Rwy'n gartref. I am home.

By Alison Wilcox (2021)

Stunning staycation: The Gower Peninsula

Covid getting you down? Longing for a holiday?

A foreign holiday may not be possible but look no further than the **staggeringly beautiful Gower Coast** for your dream destination. An **Area of Outstanding Natural Beauty with Blue Flag beaches,** and only a short drive down the M4, it is **a jewel on the Welsh coast to rival any continental resort.**

Picture hidden coves overlooked by the ruins of an ancient castle; dramatic craggy cliffs, and crystal-clear waves lapping on the shore. Imagine the warmth of the golden silky sand between your toes. Experience a walk along the Sea Serpent and follow in the footsteps of Dylan Thomas, one of Wales' iconic poets.

An historical treasure trove, the Gower boasts a genuine shipwreck, Neolithic remains, and, according to legend, is the final resting of King Arthur. Visit his burial chamber marked by one of Wales' most famous prehistoric monuments.

A surfer's paradise, an adventurer's playground, with abseiling, paragliding, mountain biking and horse riding, and much more; there is something for everyone.

For nature enthusiasts, learn about bushcraft or follow the coastal path with its breathtaking views from the dramatic clifftops.

We all need something to look forward to in these grim times. Visit our website or call the number shown below and secure a stunning staycation in the Gower Peninsula. Guaranteed to rival anything you could find across the seas.

www.gowerwow.wl

Tel. No. 01792 111 111

I'll Call Mammy

My voice is drowned out,
by the noise in the room.

I may be quiet; appear strong.
But I have feelings; I have worries.
I care; I cry.

Don't be fooled by the mask.
Don't be taken in by the silence.

If you cut me, I will bleed.
I get wounded by words.
I get bruised by actions.

I replay those words.
I relive those actions.

When I'm on my own:
When I'm in bed:
When others share **their** thoughts.

But who should I turn to?
Who can I turn to?
To share my thoughts and worries.

To say it's okay to be vulnerable:
To say it's okay to make mistakes.

To tell me –
I care; I'll listen.
I can help; I will help.

I call my mammy.

Who holds the ladder,
for me to climb.

Who erects the scaffolding,
should I slip.

Who clasps the safety-net,
should I plummet.

Who lifts me back up,
onto the ladder.

Who is always –
On the other end of the phone.

By Alison Wilcox (2019)

Floodland

Found Poem by Alison Wilcox, drawing from the novel by Marcus Sedgwick

Rising seas.
Deserted streets and derelict buildings.
Running for my life.

Body screaming, gasping.
Can't stop, get away!
Hot on my heels.

Pounding feet closing in.
Storming down the hill.
Weaving in and out.

Wet mud, sodden grass,
Slip, sprawl, slide,
Scramble and stagger to the boat

Keep going –
Look behind – stomach twists:
No-one to trust

Clamber on board, pull on the oars
No sign of land
A creeping fear

Hot sun, beating down
Dizzy, faint – slumped over the oars
Head into the unknown

By Alison Wilcox (2019)

The Sock Thief

A Moment of Frustration

"Miss, why do you always wear different coloured socks?"

"Why indeed! It's because of the sock thief, Adam."

First, the socks go into the washing basket. Then, they are loaded into the washing machine. Next, they are unloaded into the dryer, and finally, into the basket ready for distribution.

I pour out the contents of the laundry basket onto the bed, sort the socks and neatly match them into pairs. Guess what? There is always one left sitting on the bed on its own. It looks at me. Why me? Why have I been singled out? Where do they go? Could it be yet another sock-stealing dog? It was easy when Geli was alive. He loved to munch on a sock, and occasionally eat it. Discovering the missing sock was a gruesome sight …

No evidence of a sock-stealer in the two recent dogs. Time to turn detective. Blaming the dog has been too easy. Check the washing machine. No odd sock. Check the dryer. No odd sock. Check the washing basket; check the laundry basket; check the drawer; check other people's drawers. No sign of the sock!

I have yet to discover the sock thief. It comes when you least expect it. I cannot predict where or when it will strike. Is there one sock-stealer or a sock-stealing gang operating in other people's houses? One thing I know, the sock-stealer has been targeting my house for many years and I've yet to catch it. Oh well, another day of odd socks!

By Alison Wilcox (2019)

Negativity in the Media

An Angry Response

The news is on in the background: like a swarm of wasps, a black brooding cloud amassing on the horizon, getting louder and louder until it's just noise and difficult to pick out any individual sound. The voices drone on and on, carrying with them a sense of foreboding: a feeling of anxiety about what will come next. Debating, disagreeing – it's depressing as their voices get louder and louder as they strive to get their message heard.

Like a hot chili soup simmering on the stove, their negativity sends a fizzing, fiery heat slithering inside to swirl in my stomach – simmering, spitting, bubbling, then boiling over. Enough! Turn it off! Slam down the pen; grab the remote control; jab at the OFF button.

Peace at last! The fiery heat seeps out of my pores: the calm after the storm.

By Alison Wilcox (2019)

Spider's web planning template

Ask the following questions	
Name each part of the picture.	
What does it look like?	
What adjective(s) can I use to describe it?	
What is it doing?	

Scene/image box plan template

Scene/image box plan		
1. Image	Close your eyes. Picture the scene. Focus on what you can see – 'the big picture.' Zoom in on a few small details.	
2. Light	Focus on the light. Is the sun bright? Is it a dull, cloudy day? Is the light fading? Are there any shadows? Describe the colours.	
3. Sounds	Focus on the sounds. Are there any voices? Rustling leaves? Sound of rain or wind? Silence? Empty, lonely, peaceful?	
4. Smells	What can you smell? What does it remind you of?	
5. Questions	Are there any questions you have about the image? Is there anything you would like to know more about?	
6. Feelings	What feelings do you have about the image?	

7. Repeating word, phrase, line	Is there a word, phrase, line that stands out as summing up the scene and your feelings?	
8. Additional	A couple of similes or metaphors to describe the image.	

Scene/image box plan model

Scene/image box plan		
1. Image	Close your eyes. Picture the scene. Focus on what you can see – 'the big picture.' Zoom in on a few small details.	Marsh spreading out to the right; groups of wild ponies; seagull shrieks; nearing the coast.
		Steep winding road up into the hills. Narrow, hedges arching over the road; rutted track, green fields shield the coast.
		Large, five-bar white gate.
		Pig pen, cow sheds, hay barn.
		Several parked cars.
		Deadly pollen.
		Two-storey farmhouse; vegetable patch – green beans, cabbages and rhubarb.
		Old oak stable door; cold, stone flagstones.
		Wooden door to the lounge – huge hearth, logs piled by the side, brass ornaments (horse and cart), two old comfy armchairs, large sofa. Family photos.
		Kitchen: huge wooden kitchen table; loaves of bread, plates of cakes, numerous cups and saucers; two huge brown teapots.

2. Light	Focus on the light. Is the sun bright? Is it a dull, cloudy day? Is the light fading? Are there any shadows? Describe the colours.	Rays of sunlight through the small window catch the glint of the brass ornaments on the shelf. Bright summer's day; vivid blue sky.
3. Sounds	Focus on the sounds. Are there any voices? Rustling leaves? Sound of rain or wind? Silence? Empty, lonely, peaceful?	Sound of raucous laughter explodes from the kitchen. Many excited voices talking over each other … excited babble.
4. Smells	What can you smell? What does it remind you of?	Baking – fresh bread, cakes and biscuits.
5. Questions	Are there any questions you have about the image? Is there anything you would like to know more about?	Why are the kids not allowed in the parlour?

6. Feelings	What feelings do you have about the image?	Familiar, family, comforting, security, happy memories.
7. Repeating word, phrase, line	Is there a word, phrase, line that stands out as summing up the scene and your feelings? Repeat it three times throughout the description.	Comforting sound Comforting sights Comforting smells
8. Additional	A couple of similes or metaphors to describe the image.	Tripods like tepees heavy with green beans. Familiar smell of baking like a long-treasured taste of home.

Fiction planning template

Template for a plot outline

Headings	First thoughts	Detail	Focus	Zoom
Main character:				
Setting(s):				
Catalyst: Object:				

Plot

Beginning: Introducing new character and setting			
Middle:			
End:			
Message:			

Fiction planning model

"Scarlett's Adventures": Plot Outline

Headings	First thoughts	Detail	Focus	Zoom
Main character:	Scarlett 8 years old Blonde hair and blue eyes	**Clothes:** colourful leggings, hoody and baseball cap, trainers.	Trainers have glow-in-the-dark laces and flashing heels. Lots of friendship bracelets on her wrist.	Could be useful weapon against one or more of the mythical creatures. Include a swim across a river.
		Athletic.	Loves **swimming and gymnastics** (somersaults and cartwheels).	
		Brave, adventurous, kind, friendly, popular, fantastic imagination.	Loves **Greeks myths.** Wants to be an **explorer.**	Remembers the story of Theseus and the Minotaur, which helps to get them out of the maze.
		Loves **horses.**	Ambition to ride in the Grand National.	Use a **centaur/unicorn** to escape 'dark wood' and return home.
		Scared of the **dark** and large spiders.	Include journey through a dark **cave.**	**Large spider** is friendly – spins a silver thread that they follow to find their way out of the maze.
		Weakness to overcome – loves reading and did like writing stories but **struggles with spelling and lacks confidence** so no longer wants to write.	Gains confidence as **solves riddles and spells out the word that is the key** to entering the dungeon where Lena's father is being held hostage.	Change: has much more confidence and **starts writing stories again.**

Setting(s):	Secret, ancient, wood	Split into two parts (1) magical, (2) **dangerous.** **Door** in tree – tunnel down into secret wood.	Journey to include: River, rickety wooden bridge, cave Volcanic cave – eruptions **Door** is a portal.	(1) Sunny, bright blue sky; Carpet of bluebells, daffodils, vivid blooms, birds (parrots), wizard, fairies, giant toadstools. (2) Towering trees, tangled undergrowth, maze, narrow, winding paths – gloomy (include mist).
Catalyst: Object:	Finds an ancient scroll – map with runic symbols. Takes her to the ancient wood.	Map with ancient, runic symbols. Includes the key to getting into the gnome's underground kingdom. Leads Scarlett to the yew tree and tunnel into secret wood.	Don't reveal how or where she found the map until the end.	Returns to book at the end: note about believing in magic.
Plot: Beginning: Introducing new character and setting	Enters magical forest. Meets Lena, an elf, whose dad has been kidnapped by gnomes and taken to the 'dark wood.'	Messy blond, short hair that sticks up. Emerald-green eyes. Pointy ears. Clothes: sparkly, pink top and billowing, rainbow-coloured trousers. Orange, heart-shaped sunglasses. Lena's father is the king of the elves.	Hasn't had a friend before. She's different to the other elves. A bit scatty and eccentric. Loves telling stories. A bit of a coward.	Lena's dad is the king of the elves. Kidnapped for ransom by the gnomes. Ransom: magic potion developed by King Darra (Lena's dad) *Think about what potion would be a dangerous weapon for the gnomes and a threat to humans.*

(Continued)

(Continued)

Headings	First thoughts	Detail	Focus	Zoom
Middle:	Scarlett goes with Lena to the dark wood – meets deadly, mythical beasts.	Crocodile-type creatures in the river. Lion-type creature in forest. Attacked by huge birds when crossing the bridge. Encounters enormous spiders in the cave.	Conquers weakness – has to solve riddles and anagrams which requires her to spell the words correctly.	Spider is friendly and very clever – hates the gnomes – spins a silver thread to lead Scarlett and Lena through the underground maze to the dungeons. Helps Scarlett to solve the riddles. *Name of spider*
End:	Rescues dad with the help of the spider and a unicorn.		Young fairy riding the centaur looks like her sister, Martha who loves fairies and anything pink and sparkly!	
End:	Scarlett returns home. Writes the story of her adventures.	Wins a national story-writing competition.	Comments from the judges: "Scarlett really brings the magical world and its creatures to life in this wonderful story of friendship and courage. It is hard to believe that the secret wood and its inhabitants don't actually exist."	The book is published – dedicated to "My friends, Lena and Martha. I will never forget you. To those of you who think you can't spell: work hard and you will master the skill. I am living proof that it can be done."

Message:	Returns the map to the flap on the cover of her *Children's Treasury of Magical Creatures*.	As she inserts the map she glances once more at the page. On it is written: "Anything is possible if you believe."	

Character prompt card

PROMPT CARDS – ATMOSPHERE

What else can she hear?

What can she see?

In front, behind, above, to the left, to the right, in the distance.

What can she smell?

Her heart raced. A sudden noise had pierced the silence: a thud and click as the key turned in the lock and the ancient, rusty hinges creaked open.

What can she touch?

Can she taste anything?

What time of day is it? Is it light, dark?

Who is she?

Why is she there? Where is she?

Is she in danger? Why? From what?

What happens next?

Alison's Book Club

I have called this Alison's Book Club rather than a recommended reading list, as the books are ones that I have read and felt had powerful themes and the ability not just to inform but to invigorate the mind, to touch the heart and to inspire –even adults.

They are also books which illustrate the power of expression to connect with and impact the reader, and, therefore, would serve as excellent stimuli for discussions, and models and scaffolds for writing. The list is intended as a starting point rather than an exhaustive resource. (I have a wish list of hundreds of books yet to be explored.)

They are an eclectic mix of biographies, memoirs, poetry, non-fiction and fiction. They are books that I would use with a writing group to stimulate discussion, but also are beautifully written. One of my favourites was *The Earth Heroes*, from which I gathered so much information of which I was previously ignorant. These true stories of courage and creativity against all the odds, seeing treasure in trash, finding opportunities in problems were very motivating.

Writers of science fiction start with the question 'What if … ?' If you look back at earlier examples of this genre, their predictions are scarily accurate. I have, therefore, included some fiction books which look at, for example, 'What if we don't take action on climate change now?' The descriptions in these books present a stark and desolate picture, and a powerful one to make us consider the possible consequences of inaction.

As the content of this book covers a wide range and age group, so the books chosen to stimulate discussion have been carefully selected to provide a broad breadth of literature using some inspirational stories and powerful writing. As the term might suggest, personal writing is unique to the individual. Likewise, choice of biographical and autobiographical texts will be down to personal choice and interests.

Wonderful books with powerful themes may be accessible to Key Stage 2 readers, but they also have the ability to touch, inform and inspire anyone, even adults. Where young readers' versions are available, this has been noted with an asterisk. For example, *Becoming; I Am Malala; Mud, Sweat, and Tears; Long Walk to*

Freedom; and *Coming to England*. Where the content and complexity of a text is suitable for older readers, these have also been labelled (11+, 12+, 13+, etc.).

I hope that you discover a book from this list that motivates you to find your words, whether it be to entertain, preserve your memories or to write about something that interests you, inspires you, excites you or an issue that you want to draw to the attention of others. In the words of Tom Stoppard, "Words are sacred. They deserve respect. If you get the right ones in the right order, you can nudge the world a little." I hope that at least one of these books inspires you to find your words and to 'nudge your world a little.'

Happy reading.

Type	Title	Author	
BIOGRAPHY	Earth Heroes	Lily Dyu	
	The Man Who Planted Trees	Jean Giono	
	Dr Wangari Maathai Plants a Forest	Eugenia Rebel Girls	
	Greta's Story	Valentina Camerini	
	Ada's Violin	Susan Hood	
	One Plastic Bag: Isatou Ceesay and the Recycling Women of Gambia	Miranda Paul	
	A Life Story: Sir David Attenborough	Lizzie Huxley-Jones	
	The Extraordinary Life of Amelia Earhart	Dr Sheila Kanani	

(Continued)

(Continued)

Type	Title	Author	
BIOGRAPHY (continued)	The Extraordinary Life of Alan Turing	Michael Lee Richardson	
True stories about children's rights	Children Who Changed the World	Marcia Williams	
	Lightning Mary	Anthea Simmons	
	Survivors	David Long	
Incredible artists, athletes and activists with disabilities	I Am Not a Label	Cerrie Burnell	
Based on the memoirs of Clotee Henley, a young black slave	My Story: A Picture of Freedom	Patricia C. McKissack	
	Hidden Figures: The True Story of Four Black Women and the Space Race	Margot Lee Shetterly	
	Not All Heroes Wear Capes	Ben Brooks	
	Stories for Boys Who Dare to Be Different	Ben Brooks	11+
AUTOBIOGRAPHY	Boy: Tales of Childhood	Roald Dahl	
	When Hitler Stole Pink Rabbit	Judith Kerr	

(Continued)

(Continued)

Type	Title	Author	
AUTOBIOGRAPHY (continued)	Can You See Me?	Libby Scott	
	Ugly	Robert Hoge	*
	Mud, Sweat and Tears	Bear Grylls	*
	Permanent Record: How One Man Exposed the Truth about Government Spying and Digital Security	Edward Snowden	*
	I Am Malala	Malala Yousafzai	*
	Becoming	Michelle Obama	*
	Long Walk to Freedom	Nelson Mandela	*
	Coming to England	Floella Benjamin	*
	Anne Frank: The Diary of a Young Girl	Anne Frank	
	The Missing	Michael Rosen	
	A Girl on Schindler's List	Rena Finder	
	You Are a Champion	Marcus Rashford	
	Diary of a Young Naturalist	Dara McAnulty	11+
	No Summit Out of Sight	Jordan Romero	12+
	Swimming to Antarctica	Lynne Cox	12+

(Continued)

(Continued)

Type	Title	Author	
AUTOBIOGRAPHY (continued)	I Will Always Write Back	Caitlin Alifirenka and Martin Ganda	12+
	Life on Air	David Attenborough	12+
	My Family and Other Animals	Gerald Durrell	12+
	Step by Step: The Life in My Journeys	Simon Reeve	12+
	Ordinary Hazards: A Memoir	Nikki Grimes	12+
	I Know Why the Caged Bird Sings	Maya Angelou	14+
	The Life and Rhymes of Benjamin Zephaniah	Benjamin Zephaniah	12+
	Burn After Writing	Rhiannon Shove	12+
HISTORY	Black and British	David Olusoga	
FICTION	Swimming Against the Storm	Jess Butterworth	
	Windrush Child	Benjamin Zephaniah	
	The Breadwinner	Deborah Ellis	
	The Boy at the Back of the Class	Onjali Q. Rauf	
	A Boy Called Hope	Lara Williamson	

(Continued)

(Continued)

Type	Title	Author	
FICTION (continued)	Oranges in No Man's Land	Elizabeth Laird	
	My Name is Parvana	Deborah Ellis	13+
	My Name is River	Emma Rea	
	Floodworld	Tom Huddlestone	
	Floodland	Marcus Sedgwick	
	City of Rust	Gemma Fowler	
	Uglies (series)	Scott Westerfield	12+
	Matched	Ally Condie	13+
	War Girls	Tochi Onyebuchi	12+
	The Light at the Bottom of the World	London Shah	12+
	Warcross	Marie Lu	13+
	Fahrenheit 451	Ray Bradbury	15+
	The Giver	Lois Lowry	14+
POETRY	I Am the Seed That Grew the Tree	Fiona Waters	
	All the Wild Wonders	Wendy Cooling	
	Overheard in a Tower Block	Joseph Coelho	

(*Continued*)

Type	Title	Author	
POETRY (continued)	Friendly Matches	Allan Ahlberg	
	Stars with Flamingo Tails	Valerie Bloom	
	Be the Change: Poems to Help You Save the World	Liz Brownlee, Matt Goodfellow and Roger Stevens	
	The Same Inside: Poems About Empathy and Friendship	Liz Brownlee, Matt Goodfellow and Roger Stevens	
	The Very Best of Paul Cookson	Paul Cookson	
	Where Zebras Go	Sue Hardy-Dawson	
	Hey World Here I Am	Jean Little	
	Aloud in My Head	JonArno Lawson	
	If I Were Other Than Myself	Sue Hardy-Dawson	
	Does Your Face Fit?	Roger Stevens	
	Reaching the Stars: Poems About Extraordinary Women and Girls	Jan Dean, Liz Brownlee, and Michaela Morgan	
	Cloud Busting	Malorie Blackman	

(*Continued*)

(*Continued*)

Type	Title	Author	
POETRY (continued)	Aloud in My Head	Edited by JonArno Lawson	
	Everything All at Once	Steve Camden	12+
	Rhythm and Poetry	Karl Nova	12+
	Talking Turkeys	Benjamin Zephaniah	11+
	Poems about Choices	Jessica Cohn	12+
	She Will Soar	Ana Sampson	12+

Research, articles, books and websites

RESEARCH

1. 'Writing for enjoyment and its link to wider writing (findings from our Annual Literacy Survey 2016),' Christina Clark and Anne Teravainen, National Literacy Trust research (2017).
2. 'Mental wellbeing, reading and writing (How children and young people's mental wellbeing is related to their reading and writing experiences),' Christina Clark and Anne Teravainen-Goff, National Literacy Trust research report (2018).
3. 'Reading and writing your way to better mental wellbeing,' Jonathan Douglas, National Literacy Trust (26th September 2018). https://medium.com/national-literacy-trust/reading-and-writing-your-way-to-better-mental-wellbeing 2c9e671b056b.
4. 'What is the research evidence on writing?' DfE (DFE-RR238). https://www.gov.uk/government/publications/what-is-the-research-evidence-on-writing.
5. 'Educational blogs and their effects on pupils' writing,' Myra Barrs and Sarah Horrocks (2014). https://www.educationdevelopmenttrust.com/EducationDevelopmentTrust/files/7e/7ef7c4ce-5de5-495f-a89c-463e1cf8177c.pdf
6. quadblogging.net.
7. https://tes.com/magazine/article/writing-hard-pupils-deserve-our-honesty-about.
8. https://www.tes.com/magazine/article/how-schools-are-getting-writing-wrong.
9. *Visible Learning for Teachers*, John Hattie (2012).
10. *The Learning Rainforest*, Tom Sherrington (2017).
11. *Mindset (How You Can Fulfil Your Potential)*, Carol S. Dweck (2017).

INTERVIEWS AND QUOTES BY PUBLISHED AUTHORS

12. https://www.booktrust.org.uk/news-and-features/features/2016/october/floella-benjamin-on-coming-to-england-and-its-impact-20-years-on/.
13. https://www.theguardian.com/lifeandstyle/2019/dec/28/michael-rosen-family-history-jewish-culture.
14. https://elizabethlaird.co.uk/hello-teachers.
15. https://thefriendlyeditor.com/2015/03/26/how-rowling-revised-harry-potter-phoenix/.
16. https://www.explorelearning.co.uk/blog/david-walliams-top-ten-writing-tips.
17. https://www.theguardian.com/childrens-books-site/2014/oct/07/Marcus-sedgwick-where-i-write-the-ghosts-of-heaven.
18. www.bbc.co.uk/sounds/play/b050z2vc (BBC Radio 4 Book Club interview with Judith Kerr).
19. https://www.bbc.co.uk/cbbc/joinin/bp-anthony-horowitz-spy-story-writing-masterclass.

EXTERNAL WRITING PROMPTS

20. www.poetrybycharlescfinn.com.

Social media

21. 'Anxiety on the rise among the young in social media age,' Robert Booth (The Guardian, 5th February 2019).
22. https://www.rsph.org.uk/static/uploaded/d125b27c-0b62-41c5-a2c0155a8887cd01.pdf.
23. 'Social media putting "overwhelming pressure" on young people,' Prince's Trust (5th February 2019).
24. 'The experiences of children aged 11–12 on social networking sites,' Ruth Ball and Claire Lilley, UKCCIS and NSPCC (2014).

25. https://www.fenews.co.uk/press-releases/31095-education-secretary-damian-hinds-is-calling-on-social-media-influencers-to-take-responsi-bility-for-their-young-audience.

Racism in sport

26. https://www.theredcard.org/education-pack.
27. https://www.theguardian.com/football/2019/oct2014/Bulgaria-england-euro-2020-qualifying-match-report.
28. www.facebook.com/499223133910599/posts/greater-manchester-police-we-are-aware-of-a-number-of-mnachester-united-football/1049552625544311/.
29. www.letsendhatecrime.com.
30. www.englandnetball.co.uk/netball-against-racism.
31. www.rugbyagainstracism.com.
32. https://www.coe.int/en/web/european-commission-against-racism-and-intolerance/recommendation-no.12.

Climate change

33. '"It's our time to rise up": youth climate strikes held in 100 countries,' Sandra Laville, Matthew Taylor and Daniel Hurst (The Guardian, 15th March 2019).
34. https://theconversation.com/fridays-for-future-how-the-young-climate-movement-has-grown-since-greta-thunbergs-lone-protest-144781.
35. www.fridaysforfuture.org.
36. *Be The Change: Poems to Help You Save the World*, Liz Brownlee, Matt Goodfellow and Roger Stevens (2019).
37. *Where Zebras Go*, Sue Hardy-Dawson (2017).
38. https://www.nature.com/articles/d41586-019-02696-0.

IDEAS AND TEXTS

39. https://www.writing4pleasure.com.
40. https://www.cressidacowell.co.uk.
41. www.poetryroundabout.com.
42. https://www.madeleinelindley.com.

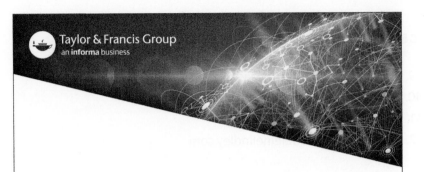

For Product Safety Concerns and Information please contact our EU
representative GPSR@taylorandfrancis.com Taylor & Francis Verlag GmbH,
Kaufingerstraße 24, 80331 München, Germany

Printed and bound by CPI Group (UK) Ltd, Croydon, CR0 4YY
11/04/2025
01843991-0003